Truths, Falsehoods, and a Wee Bit of Honesty:

A Short Primer on the Prose Poem with Selected Letters from Russell Edson

TRUTHS, FALSEHOODS, AND A WEE BIT OF HONESTY:
A SHORT PRIMER ON THE PROSE POEM WITH SELECTED LETTERS FROM RUSSELL EDSON

Peter Johnson

MadHat Press
Cheshire, Massachusetts

MadHat Press
Cheshire, Massachusetts

Copyright © 2020 Peter Johnson
All rights reserved

The Library of Congress has assigned
this edition a Control Number of
2020950126

ISBN 978-1-952335-14-3 (paperback)

Cover art and design by Marc Vincenz
Book design by MadHat Press
Author photo by Genevieve Allaire Johnson

www.madhat-press.com

First Printing

*For Martin Pops, Charles Simic, and Gary Lindberg,
early mentors and very classy guys*

A Brief Note on the Selections

Over the years I've written many short essays and book reviews on the prose poem, but for this volume I decided not to include the book reviews and instead focus mostly on my short essays that deal specifically with the prose poem as a genre and the unique possibilities it offers. Russell Edson used to say that the problem with most contemporary poetry was that it was characterized by "too much language chasing too little of an idea." Much the same could be said about contemporary literary criticism, so I decided not to add to the problem.

Long live the prose poem, whatever the hell it is!

Table of Contents

Essays

Truths, Falsehoods, and a Wee Bit of Honesty	3
The Prose Poem and the Problem of Genre	7
The Prose Poem and the Comic: On Russell Edson's "The Manual of Sleep"	15
Parable vs. Prose Poem: Lawrence Fixel's "Flight Patterns"	21
Introduction to *Sentence: A Journal of Prose Poetics,* Volume 4	27
My Ten Favorite Books, At Least for This Week	31

Interviews

The Art of the Prose Poem: Interview with Russell Edson	37
The Art of the Prose Poem: Interview with Robert Bly	53
Interview with Peter Johnson by Steve Frech	71
Interview with Peter Johnson by David Cass	79
Interview with Peter Johnson by Jamey Dunham	89

Selected Letters from Russell Edson

Little Mr. Prose Poem	103
Selected Annotated Letters from Russell Edson	105

If Catullus Were a Prose Poet

If Catullus Were a Prose Poet	173
Acknowledgments	177
About the Author	179

Essays

Truths, Falsehoods, and a Wee Bit of Honesty

My favorite passage in literature comes from the introductory section of *Winesburg, Ohio,* called "The Book of the Grotesque." In this section, an unnamed narrator tells of an "old man" who lists "hundreds of truths" in his book. There is the "truth of virginity, the truth of passion, the truth of wealth and poverty, of thrift and of profligacy, of carelessness and abandon. Hundreds and hundreds were the truths, and they were beautiful." A transitional sentence follows which, to me, explains much about human nature. After mentioning these "truths," the narrator says, "And then the people came along."

> Each as he appeared snatched up one of the truths and some who were quite strong snatched up a dozen of them. It was the truths that made people grotesques. The old man had quite an elaborate theory concerning the matter. It was his notion that the moment one of the people took one of the truths to himself, called it his truth, and tried to live his life by it, he became a grotesque and the truth he embraced became a falsehood.

Politics in the literary world involves negotiating these kinds of "truths," which usually manifest themselves as prejudices or obsessions. Certainly, we prose poets face obstacles unique to our calling, but most of our problems are the same ones verse poets confront. For one thing, even the best of editors embrace certain truths (how can they not?), which can make them grotesque. Some editors also walk point for different literary movements, and the great irony has always been that the more avant-garde a movement pretends to be—self-consciously pitting itself against a real or imagined Tradition—the more it resembles the snobbiest of country clubs, whose mottos have always been, "Exclude, Exclude, Exclude." But at least most editors and movements seem dedicated to their truths—almost on a mission. And there's a certain honesty to that.

The real problems occur when the truths editors embrace are changeable and determined by career moves—"career" being a word I hear all the time and find very curious when mentioned in the same breath with poetry. When I first began submitting poems, I imagined sophisticated, open-minded editors sitting in spacious, book-lined studies, reading my poems, then setting them aside, only to return later to savor their deeper resonances. After eight years of running a literary magazine, I now know that any meathead can be an editor. I'm the perfect example. All you need is a minimal amount of money to print a small volume. Or, even easier, you can hover around an established journal and wait for the editors to die off. And there is a career track, every bit as delineated as the one at Goldman Sachs—solicit and publish the big-name poets; anticipate who the new movers-and-groovers will be; and publish or write book reviews for all of them. Also, send them frequent and obsequious letters. Even if they think you're a dope, they'll want to hear nice things about themselves. Within five years, you may find yourself sitting in your favorite coffee shop, sharing a tiramisu with the Poet Laureate.

In spite of this political nonsense, poets who care about their work will continue to write and to submit. Witness prose poets, who have more problems to deal with than the average poet. For one thing, some editors—though not as many as there used to be—either hate prose poetry, or don't think it exists. Publication of prose poems also depends on an editor's knowledge of the genre, and some may not be well versed in any kind of prose-poem tradition, or be open to the genre's endless possibilities. Consequently, if you're trying to do something very different, you may end up being the best, least-read prose poet of your generation. But if we begin to feel too sorry for prose poets, we should realize that many of them create their own problems by calling their prose poems, at any given time, short-short stories, parables, fables, and so on. Russell Edson has said, "What name one gives or doesn't give to his or her writing is far less interesting than the work itself." True, yet we *do* make a political decision when we consciously choose to write poems in prose instead of in verse, and when we subsequently decide to call a finished product a prose poem or a short-short story.

Of course, there are no solutions to the political in-fighting in the literary world, which fact gives us permission to whine endlessly when our work is rejected. This is good for the soul, and we should keep in mind that this year's biggest whiner is very often next year's superstar. Nevertheless, I do think that we could create a better literary climate if we would become more honest and organized about our politics. For example, every literary movement could be run like a political party, and every poet could be made to join one of these parties. To show my good faith, as of today, I am officially founding the "Prose Poem Party." It will include both living and dead authors. Russell Edson will be the President and Maxine Chernoff his First Lady, with Rimbaud their *enfant terrible*. All prose poets will move to Why, Arizona, where we'll create our own state. Our constitution will be the preface to *Paris Spleen*. The State mascot will be the platypus; the State seal, a question mark. Any prose poet refusing to join the Party will be banished to Bread Loaf without a tennis racket. Our literary journal will be called *Linear—Sometimes,* and its content, except for the editor's name, will be published in invisible ink. You will have to read our journal backwards; you will have to read it blindfolded. Solicited poems will be returned unread; unsolicited ones will be glanced at between 4:00 and 4:05 p.m. on January 13th. Please no prose poems about mothers, fathers, children, flowers, or sex acts. Definitely no working-class poems.

So let it be written.

So let it be done.

The Prose Poem and the Problem of Genre

When it comes to deciding on whether a work of short prose is a prose poem, a flash fiction, a microessay, or any other short genre you can think up, no one seems to care anymore. "Forget about genre," people say, "All that matters, is if the piece is any good." Well, of course, but these same people forget to mention that what's good is often very subjective. Many people love the prose in *Tender Buttons*. I too appreciate Stein's wit and intelligence, but I can't say I enjoy reading the book. To me, it's like going to bed with someone who wants to discuss Wittgenstein all night. "Yeah, fascinating stuff," you say, "but when are we going to get to the fun part?" So does "good" have to do with the artistic appreciation of what an author is attempting, or does it refer to the pure enjoyment of the text without knowing anything about genre or literary precedents or autobiographical details, or what the author says about his or her work?

What makes a discussion of the prose poem-as-genre even more confusing is that it has a long history of borrowing from other genres, and it often does this playfully. The prose poem likes to have fun, and to most poets poetry is a very serious business. To simplify matters, I'd like to begin by accepting the notion that it is impossible to define the prose poem, which doesn't mean that issues of genre are irrelevant. The best we can do is to argue that the prose poem exhibits certain characteristics, and even those characteristics are determined by the literary background and tastes of the person reading the prose poem. Any approach to it as a genre must necessarily be eclectic. When pressed, my go-to description of prose poetry is Michael Benedikt's. He writes that prose poetry "is a genre of poetry, self-consciously written in prose, and characterized by the intense use of virtually all the devices of poetry, which includes the intense use of devices of verse," except for the line break. This description works for me because it privileges the "poetry" part of the genre, and it's broad enough to be fairly inclusive.

What I'd like to do is to offer brief personal readings of three very different works of prose that I consider to be prose poetry. After that's done, I'll make a few generalizations that will annoy everyone. Let it be known that the following readings are offered by a guy who writes prose poetry, exclusively, who has read the major studies of the genre, who founded a journal on the prose poem and edited it for nine years, who has been sent and has read about 150 books of prose poetry, who taught a course on the prose poem for twenty years, and who recently finished editing an anthology where he asked eighty contemporary American poets to choose a prose poem and to write a commentary on it.

And now the poems:

Clear of oak groves, sunrise stretched a thin reach deep into the chamber, tripping the setting of fires on hilltops: signals relayed to the quarters. A day to plant or hunt, enter women or agreements.

Night skies were laid on fields in perfect orientation before the plates opened, wandered, collided; they continue and will. There is so much to take into account. It may be impossible to choose for myself; all pleasures might hand me loneliness.

I find the dark room, tip the white table to catch a shaft bent by a mirror, shot through a pin hole, and I'll watch the ocean upside down. Foam churns at the edge of a vision. It is time to do something in particular.

—*Killarney Clary*

I was stolen by the gypsies. My parents stole me right back. Then the gypsies stole me again. This went on for some time. One minute I was in the caravan suckling the dark teat of my new mother, the next I sat at the long dining room table eating my breakfast with a silver spoon.

It was the first day of spring. One of my fathers was singing in the bathtub; the other one was painting a live sparrow the colors of a tropical bird.

—*Charles Simic*

I worried about the gap between expression and intent, afraid the world might see a fluorescent advertisement where I meant to show a face. Sincerity is no help once we admit to the lies we tell on nocturnal occasions, even in the solitude of our own heart, wishcraft slanting the naked figure from need to seduce to fear of possession. Far better to cultivate the gap itself with its high grass for privacy and reference gone astray. Never mind that it is not philosophy, but raw electrons jumping from orbit to orbit to ready the pit for the orchestra, scrap meanings amplifying the succession of green perspective, moist fissures, spasms on the lips.

—*Rosmarie Waldrop*

Killarney Clary's untitled piece is the perfect poem in prose. It has a recognizable prose narrative structure, but because of its internal leaps, normal narrative syntax is subverted. Thus, the leaps act like line breaks in verse. Throughout the poem, poetic descriptions are often followed by statements. Consider this poem without those statements:

> Clear of oak groves, sunrise stretched a thin reach deep into the chamber, tripping the setting of fires on hilltops. Night skies were laid on fields in perfect orientation before the plates opened, wandered, collided. I find the dark room, tip the white table to catch a shaft bent by a mirror, shot through a pin hole, and I'll watch the ocean upside down. Foam churns at the edge of a vision.

On its own, this is a very fine prose poem, containing many characteristics we associate with verse poetry. It has figurative language and the kind of "I" we find in lyric poetry. How often have natural descriptions, from the time of the Romantics, mirrored the internal state of the poet? But the poem gains more complexity with the addition of those discursive statements: "There is so much to take into account. It may be impossible to choose for myself"; "all pleasures might hand me loneliness"; and "It is time to do something in particular." These statements provide the leaps and juxtapositions between discourses so characteristic of prose poetry. To borrow a description of prose poetry from Charles Simic, it seems that Clary's piece "looks like prose on the page, but acts like a poem in your head."

My reading of Clary's piece is also influenced by other knowledge about prose poetry I've absorbed over the years. The first time I read Clary's poem I appreciated its poetic language and interesting shifts in consciousness that made its meaning elusive. But then I began to situate it in a tradition. I saw it in the context of the associative leaps that Robert Bly says characterize prose poetry. Much of the deep imagery in Clary's poem even approximates the spirituality of Bly's best object prose poems. Her poem reminds me, too, of the austerity of Jean Follain's prose poems. Both poets are exceptional at recreating what Follain calls, "a world rich in anniversaries." Was Clary inspired by Follain or Bly? Was she also influenced by the very short epiphanic moments of her friend Gary Young's prose poetry, who himself was influenced by Bashō's haikus? Are Clary's prose poems, in a way, extended prose haikus? Who knows? What matters is that once a prose poem is written it becomes part of a genre tradition, and knowing that tradition affects how we read and evaluate it, and that evaluation changes over time.

Does it help, too, knowing that Clary's poem was submitted and first appeared in a journal on the prose poem, and later appeared in a book that was published and marketed as a book of prose poems? Of course.

Charles Simic's piece is a very different animal, though, in some ways, easier to evaluate as a prose poem. Ignoring genre for a second, we can see many of the classic traits found in Simic's verse poetry. He starts with an odd first sentence, then follows its logic, a strategy that, as in Russell Edson's prose poems, often creates humor. Simic's interest in folktales is also here. He seems to have fun flipping the prince-and-the-pauper genre on its head. Instead of there being two narrators who choose to change places, Simic's narrator involuntarily lives a double life, endlessly being stolen, and then stolen back. This kind of repetition and juxtaposition also creates humor. Look at Edson's prose poem "The Captain" to see a similar example of how this kind of repetition works.

It seems, then, that it helps to read Simic's poem if we come to it with the above knowledge. But there's more! Simic has actually written on prose poetry, calling it a "veritable literary hybrid, an impossible amalgamation of lyric poetry, anecdote, fairy tale, allegory, joke, journal entry, and many other kinds of prose." This sounds to me like a perfect description of "I was stolen by the gypsies." To make things easier he's even confessed that while writing the poem he was thinking about the "brevity and stunning lunacy" of the prose poems of Max Jacob, Daniil Kharms, and Russell Edson. Even the book that the poem appeared in, *The World Doesn't End,* was published, marketed, and received the Pulitzer Prize as a book of prose poems, much to the horror of many verse poets.

With all this information in mind, it would be difficult not to read "I was stolen by the gypsies" as a prose poem, or to evaluate it in the context of the other prose poems and genres Simic mentions. But not so fast! In a commentary on this poem, Simic confesses that the "prose fragments" in *The World Doesn't End* were never meant to be labeled prose poetry. "What I had done," he writes, "is to copy some of my nearly illegible scribblings from old notebooks, which after I rediscovered them and read them, struck me as having poetic qualities of their own and strung all together surprisingly read like a tongue-in-cheek autobiography [yet another genre]." But his editor insisted that they had to call the book something, so she and Simic settled upon prose poetry.

Should we care about this revelation? Does it change the way we read and evaluate the fragments in *The World Doesn't End?* I'll try to make sense of this later.

Coming to Rosmarie Waldrop's piece with no knowledge of her or the milieu she operates in can be very frustrating. Meaning is very elusive. We have the lyric "I" but it's very different from Killarney Clary's "I." Waldrop's "I" is more ruminative. On the first reading, the piece seems deliberately obscure, even mean-spirited in the way it thumbs its nose at referentiality. We are used to being spoon-fed poetry, and even when we come upon a difficult poem, there are usually recognizable metaphors to guide us. In contrast, we have to read Waldrop's poem in a whole new way. The key sentence is: "Far better to cultivate the gap itself with its high grass for privacy and reference gone astray." Thus, the poem itself is a defense of the method and sensibility informing the poem. Waldrop herself is "worried" that people might not "get" the poem, but she ends up feeling that it's better and more authentic to cultivate the "gaps," which will lead us to a new way of reading poetry and of experiencing the world.

This interpretation is borne out by Waldrop's own comments on the poem. First, she argues that the prose poem should not be confused with fiction. "Of the two terms yoked together in its name," she writes, "*poem* is the more important. It needs to have the poem's density and intensity. It must take wing." She goes on to say that in her prose poems, "I cultivate cuts, discontinuity, leaps, shifts in reference. 'Gap gardening,' I have called it, and my main tool for it is collage." Perhaps it might be best to describe Waldrop's poem, and much of Language poetry-in-prose for that matter, as exploratory prose, which often appeals more to the intellect than to the emotions.

As in the case of Simic and Clary, Waldrop's poem was published as a sequence of prose poems and marketed as such. She also edited Burning Deck Press for years, which published many seminal books of prose poems, especially from writers abroad. This information must also affect our reception of the poem.

So where does all of this leave us? I would suggest the following common-sense generalizations (at least to me) about how to read prose poetry.

1. Any formal definition of the prose poem fails. Description should be privileged over prescription. In his study of the

prose poem, Michel Delville provides us with one possible interpretive strategy: "to draw inductively on an existing body of works labeled, marketed, or simply received as prose poems."
2. It is impossible to look at the prose poem outside of the context of other genres that it shares traits with or subverts. We can't come to a work as blank slates. We bring our knowledge of other genres with us, even if we have absorbed those genres unconsciously. In terms of the prose poem, fables, fairy tales, riddles, and folktales come to mind.
3. Extraliterary information can be helpful. Even what an author says is useful. Even if an author says that his short prose wasn't self-consciously written as prose poetry, that information helps us in evaluating a work. Take Simic's case, for example. Although he suggests that he never expected his prose fragments to be received as prose poems, he does admit that he's always been a fan of the prose poetry of Max Jacob, Daniil Kharms, and Russell Edson. Perhaps, then, he has unconsciously adopted some of their strategies in his fragments: the unexpected juxtapositions that cause humor, for instance. And even if he hasn't, once he mentions those writers, it is fruitful to revisit the prose poems in *The World Doesn't End* with those writers in mind.
4. The connections between genre and interpretation and evaluation are important. As Steve Monte says, "'What does it mean to read X as a prose poem?' may turn out to be a more significant question than 'Is X a prose poem?'" Later he adds, that when "we try to decide the genre of a work, then, our aim is to discover its meaning." Some of Picasso's Cubist paintings viewed out of context are unintelligible. But when we discover that one is called "Still Life with a Bottle of Rum," suddenly previously enigmatic lines and angles make sense, and the painting can be partially evaluated by how it adds to or subverts the still life genre.
5. All of the above is negotiable and fluid. Or as Monte writes, "Our sense of genre is therefore always 'in progress,'

changing as we read onward and encounter new interpretive frameworks." It is, in fact, this dynamic quality of the prose poem, always straddling the lines between poetry and prose and the borders between genres, both feet planted precariously on banana peels, that makes it so appealing.

So to all who say, "Forget about genre. All that matters is if a work is any good," I say "Hooey!" Statements like these privilege the reader to an absurd degree, while also being an example of the kind of narcissistic, lazy thinking responsible for much of the weak criticism and poetry being written today.

The Prose Poem and the Comic: On Russell Edson's "The Manual of Sleep"

Kierkegaard wrote that the "comical is present in every stage of life, for wherever there is life there is contradiction." Although even the biggest sourpuss might agree with this statement, anyone who has ever taught a course on comedy knows that it's very difficult to decide just what is comic. In my dissertation on black humor in the novels of John Hawkes I went to great lengths to describe the dark comedy of a scene in *The Lime Twig* where a woman is bound by a thug, appropriately named Thick, then beaten to death with a truncheon. I showed how Hawkes distances us from the event by narrating it through the point of view of the woman, who, at the moment of the beating, is considering, among other odd things, how the position she's tied in is bad for her figure.

Imagine my shock when one of my readers, a woman of course, angrily pointed out that there never was and never would be anything funny about a woman being violently murdered. Was she just a humorless feminist? Not at all. In fact, by any decent moral standards, she was right, yet wasn't she missing Hawkes's point and letting her moral qualms obscure her literary judgment?

It does seem that comedy shares the same problem as pornography. As D. H. Lawrence said, "What is pornography to one man is the laughter of genius to another." Teach Woody Allen's short fiction to a class of freshman; some will laugh so hard they'll nearly fall off their chairs; others will find him stupid and silly. Teach a few classes on the literary and artistic experiments of Dada; some will rejoice in its nihilistic hijinks, others will find them incoherent, childish, or needlessly obscure—all of which responses, ironically, would have pleased the Dadaists.

This lack of consensus on comedy was driven home to me about eight years ago when I was still editing *The Prose Poem: An International Journal.* Russell Edson had sent me a number of prose poems, and I was trying to decide which ones to accept. One of the poems was called "The Encounter."

> A hand was resting on the table in front of me in a sleepy fist. Suddenly it flipped on its back and opened its fingers as if asking to have its palm read.
>
> But as I looked into its lines it suddenly flew up and slapped me in the face.
>
> I began to cry ...
>
> Then this hand, I forget which, began to wipe away my tears ...

A cute poem, but certainly not one of Edson's strongest, so I placed it on the end table and began paging through his other submissions. At that moment my nine-year-old son stumbled in, grabbed the poem, and read it, whereupon he broke into uncontrollable laughter. What did he see that I didn't? And his reaction was important because I was editing a journal and teaching a course on prose poetry, and the prose poem from *Paris Spleen* onward often veers toward the comic. In fact, the majority of the submissions I received were comic poems, or at least attempted to be so.

Why does the prose poem have a generic predisposition toward comedy?

Here are a few thoughts on the subject.

Kierkegaard's emphasis on contradiction is certainly important. What can be more contradictory than a poem in prose, with its oxymoronic name and paradoxical nature? Edson alludes to this inherent contradiction, comparing the prose poem to a "cast-iron aeroplane that can actually fly." Charles Simic notes the slapstick element in its composition when he writes: "Writing a prose poem is a bit like trying to catch a fly in a dark room. The fly probably isn't even there, the fly is inside your head, still you keep tripping over and bumping into things in hot pursuit." One reason for the recent prose-poem renaissance is that the postmodern is the norm, almost a cliché. We're not surprised to see a bald, fully tattooed young woman with three nose rings walking down the street, reading the sermons of Cotton Mather, wearing a Versace blouse, cutoff jeans, and a pair of wingtips. That's the spirit of the prose poem, which is why it flourished during the periods of Dada and surrealism and during the collage experiments of the Cubists. It's only appropriate that Max Jacob shared living space with Picasso. And what better approximates the comic juxtaposition and disruption of the prose poem, not to mention its parodic inclinations, than a work like Duchamp's *The Bride,* which visually debunks one of the sacred symbols of romantic love by splintering planes and connecting shifting forms with odd pipes and tendons, forcing us to yoke two different and opposed views of the human anatomy.

Arthur Koestler calls this interpretive act "bisociation." He begins his discussion by referring to a joke from Freud's essay on the unconscious, a joke that reads like a prose poem:

> Chamfort tells the story of a Marquis at the court of Louis XIV who, on entering his wife's boudoir and finding her in the arms of the Bishop, walked calmly to the window and went through the motion of blessing the people in the street.
> "What are you doing?" cried the angry wife.
> "Monsignor is performing my functions," replied the Marquis, "so I am performing his."

Koestler attributes the humor of this joke to the Marquis' unexpected reaction, which overthrows our own expectations. But more important, he argues that we laugh at the joke because it contains two separate and self-consistent "frames of reference," in this case "codes of conduct." The logic of one code of behavior suggests that the Marquis will be so angered that he might throw the Bishop out of the window. But, simultaneously, we recognize another code, which deals with the "division of labor, the quid pro quo, the give and take." And this code, too, has its own logic, which makes sense to us in another context. The "clash of these two mutually incompatible codes or associative contexts" can best be seen in a prose poem like Edson's "Sleep":

> There was a man who didn't know how to sleep, nodding off every night into a drab unprofessional sleep. Sleep that he'd grown so tired of sleeping.
>
> He tried reading *The Manual of Sleep,* but it just put him to sleep. That same old sleep that he had grown so tired of sleeping …
>
> He needed a sleeping master, who with a whip and chair would discipline the night, and make him jump through hoops of gasolined fire. Someone who could make a tiger sit on a tiny pedestal and yawn.

We laugh at this poem because of the juxtaposition of the simple, hopefully natural act of sleeping with the stern discipline we associate with manuals and circus trainers. The comic absurdity of the poem is captured with the phrase "sleeping master." Yet the poem is held together by its "logic of composition," a phrase Edson uses to describe his poems. Certainly, if there is such a thing as "unprofessional sleep," then there must be "*The Manual of Sleep*" and a "sleeping master." Now you might ask, "Couldn't a verse poem manipulate some of these same conceits?" Most certainly, yet I believe that the paradoxical nature of the prose poem, the way it so willingly embraces opposites, makes it a fertile place for such bisociation, which is why so many comic sensibilities are attracted to it.

But this process of bisociation is not a tidy act, one that can be diagrammed on a graph, accompanied by a clear resolution, as certain theorists of comedy would like us to believe. These critics often attempt to freeze the comic moment, then point to its social significance. According to this approach, "Sleep" would be a satire on the artificial and mechanical ways humans attempt to deal with a natural problem. Edson's insomniac would be a perfect example of a person trying to encrust the mechanical onto the living—to paraphrase Henri Bergson's description of comedy. Edson himself would groan at this kind of reading, arguing that he is not interested in satire but in the "shape of thought." Perhaps this is what Fred Miller Robinson means when, referring to Bergson, he writes:

> What is "encrusted" on us, the living, is our intellect, which perceives in fixed products a reality that is in constant process. The natural, the adaptable, the pliable, the creative, are not strictly social ideals, but the very life of things. So that when we discover the comic, we are not always correcting mechanical behavior, but we can be observing an aspect of human behavior that is beyond correction, that is universal.

Prose poetry, I think, privileges "the natural, the adaptable, the pliable." It is the wild card of literary genres, where process and possibility are more important than representation. Elsewhere I have compared the genre-blending nature of the prose poem to the platypus, which is an egg-laying mammal with webbed feet, a beaver-like tail, and a duckbill. Certainly, the blending of these unlike characteristics makes us laugh at the platypus, just as we are amused by the way prose poems merge elements of the parable, the fable, the aphorism, the pensée and so on. But, unlike the prose poem's indeterminate generic makeup, the platypus's genetic code is predetermined. It can't all of a sudden grow an elephant's trunk out of its backside, or a rhinoceros's horn out of its forehead, then have a Venus flytrap sprout from the tip of the horn. If it could endlessly reinvent itself like this, then it would resemble a prose poem, and a pretty good one at that.

Parable or Prose Poem: Lawrence Fixel's "Flight Patterns"

After the literary dust of the last fifty years settles and some academic has the nerve to write the history of the American prose poem from 1965 onward, when trying to canonize the most important figure of that period that academic will have a long line of fine poets to choose from. But if that history were also to include the parable, I would argue that there's only one writer and one collection that stands above the others. That writer is Lawrence Fixel, and that collection is *Truth, War, and the Dream-Game: Selected Prose Poems and Parables, 1966–1990* (Coffee House Press, 1991).

In his "Foreword" to *Truth, War, and the Dream-Game* (hereafter referred to as *TWD*) Fixel himself makes a distinction between the prose poem and the parable, saying,

> ... the parable is required to be *about something*—something that connects with, even though it conflicts with, our sense of the world. Thus it challenges our assumptions while, paradoxically, it evokes some feeling of universality. The prose poem ... tends to be lyrical, subjective, impressionistic. Based more on self-expression than the concept of metaphor offered by the parable, it can provide a counterpoint of *possibility* to balance the parable's greater concern with *necessity.*

What Fixel says about the prose poem is true, but I am mostly interested in his parables, which he further discusses in his "Foreword."

In contrast to the "ancient moralistic parable," which sometimes appears as a "riddle or an enigma," Fixel posits the "modern parable."

According to him, this parable, exemplified in the works of Kafka and Borges, offers a "devastating illumination of a world split between psyche, spirit, and material concerns." He adds that in this kind of parable, "paradox is a key element, opposing the identity of opposites to any commonsense, linear, or literal world."

Another way of describing this modern parable is to call it an "open parable," a phrase Roy Pascal applies to Kafka's parables. Making a contrast between fables and Kafka's short works, Pascal writes:

> Although Kafka invites us to read his parables with the same expectation of a simple moral lesson that will illuminate the meaning of the events related, in fact the reader finds his expectations cheated, for there is no formulated moral and the conclusion of the incident is obscure and ambiguous, leaving the reader baffled and depressed.... The essence of the fable or parable is precisely of a clear, defined moral influence or injunction; and here, in Kafka's parables, this essence is absent.... The function of fable was to allow us to understand life, to order and label its manifestations, to teach us practical wisdom that will serve to guide our behavior. But Kafka's fables do not illuminate the mind but terrify and confuse.

I mention the above distinctions because they provide a lens through which we can view and experience Fixel's parables, and we should keep these distinctions in mind when looking at the first parable in *TWD*, called "Flight Patterns"—a prose piece that prepares us for all of the others that follow.

Flight Patterns

Between the void and the sheer event....
　　—Valéry

1.
It is said, of the millions that undertake the journey, that the greatest number are lost somewhere along the way. To prove this, evidence is produced, statistics gathered, witnesses summoned. There are even films of the long, straggling procession, which presumably reveal the fate of the missing. Yet it appears no one—ourselves

included—is deterred by this, for it is equally intolerable to remain where we are.

2.
… Word continues to arrive from monitors at the highly equipped tracking stations. They report a whole series of unexplained dots and dashes on the flickering screens. Even the most experienced observers—using the most advanced techniques—concede that the habitual flight patterns can no longer be interpreted….

3.
I have seen some of the incoming messages. They bear such strange notations as "missing in action," "dead on arrival," etc. With so many different languages, from such different worlds, the gap between what is transmitted and received continues to widen.

4.
I have resolved not to be upset by any of this. To limit myself to what can be verified by sensory evidence. One thing is clear, whether we travel the direct route of desire, or detours of illusion, we still miss connection. Something is there—ahead or behind us—and we are drawn in that direction. For a time we seem to have arrived…. But as the wind changes, the mist descends, we can no longer tell where we are.

5.
Let us suppose, for instance, that you have been where I have been. We meet one afternoon in a neighboring country…. Joining the crowd in the plaza, we observe the stately walk of the costumed women. Moving on, we notice in contrast the immobility of the vendors: the heavy bodies squatting beside earthen jars.

6.
Is the scene familiar? Then let memory take a further step: to that moment when armed men in gray uniforms appear…. Suddenly we feel a sharp intersection of competing gestures, of inviting and

disturbing fragrances. Someone drops petals in front of the candle-lit altar; someone else throws poisoned meat to the hungry dogs.... Speaking of this later, disturbed by our fragmented impressions, the question arises: What name can we give to this land?

7.
We may of course continue the search, each producing letters, photographs, documents. Or simply recognize that, between any two witnesses, we can expect these differences. Each might then retreat into a private retrospect.... But what if we decide to give up these wanderings, returning to this body, this present time? It may then occur to us that what signifies this world is nothing else but the current of our feeling. And as for the flesh that dissolves, disappears, who can say it will not appear again? If not in this form, this familiar image, then perhaps as an *intention* that moves through silence and the quickening wind.

"Flight Patterns"—What a wonderfully ironic title, juxtaposing both the freedom and uncertainty of taking wing with the certainty of a preconceived pattern, which we may choose to follow so we don't get lost. It's an ideal position to be in, but one that, ironically, Fixel's parables always argue against, since no matter how hard his narrator tries to find a fixed location from which to make sense of his surroundings, uncertainty prevails. It's appropriate, then, that "Flight Patterns" begins with this Kafkaesque opening: "It is said, of the millions who undertake the journey, that the greatest number are lost somewhere along the way." Still, the narrator adds, we persist because "it is equally intolerable to remain where we are."

Any physical journey presumes the presence of signposts, which in literary journeys correspond to symbols. But in Fixel's parables symbols are often difficult, if not impossible, to read because they appear as "sharp intersection[s] of competing gestures." Throughout "Flight Patterns," no course of action is explicitly suggested, and every possible revelation is undercut with qualifiers. Films "*presumably* [italics mine] reveal the fate of the missing"; there are "unexplained dots and dashes on the flickering screens"; and "the most experienced observers—using the most advanced techniques—concede that the habitual flight patterns can no longer be interpreted...." Even the narrator's persistent use of ellipses suggests that just when we are about to ease into a comfortable intellectual or moral position, just when we may have a chance to "give [a name] to this land," our hopes for success unwind in a series of dots, so that the "gap between what is submitted and received continues to widen." Ultimately, all traditional symbols, along with other traditional signifiers, remain untranslatable.

Pretty dismal stuff, except that just as we are about to hang our heads in existential despair, section four begins with a surprising and quietly comic assertion: "I have resigned myself not to be upset by any of this." This is an important moment in "Flight Patterns." In spite of uncertainty, the narrator claims that the "flight" is still worth it, not just in this poem but in all the prose poems and parables that will follow. He also offers to be our guide, while again reminding us that the journey will not be easy, because "whether we travel the direct route of desire, or detours of illusion, we will still miss connection," and just "as the wind changes, the mist descends, we can no longer tell where we are."

I would argue that in Fixel's parables, being situated in this no man's land is not a bad thing. In fact, it's the only thing, and it has its advantages. We should remember Kafka's description of that moment between sleeping and waking, which he calls the "riskiest moment of the day." The narrator of "Flight Patterns" seems to suggest that this risk is necessary, and in the last section of the poem he even gives us a manual of sorts. He admits that we can keep "producing" what we mistakenly believe to be definitive texts, like "letters, photographs, documents," and then "retreat into private retrospect" to endlessly examine them. But maybe there is a better way. "Wonder," he writes, "if we decide to give up these [speculative] wanderings, returning to this body, this present time? It may then occur to us that what signifies this world is nothing else but the current of our feeling."

This is where I think Fixel's parables differ from Kafka's. Fixel asserts our strength as individuals, even as he accepts the incomprehensibility that Kafka so intricately praises and damns in "On Parables." Like his fellow WPA poet, David Ignatow, Fixel embraces a guarded optimism. We should take heart because, as he suggests in another prose poem/parable, called "Above It All," "Even now someone is at work in a garage, a small shed, to find a solution.... Some morning soon, a figure will appear on a roof, waiting to lift off. Not an apparition, I assure you, but someone like ourselves...."

Someone, of course, like Lawrence Fixel.

Introduction to *Sentence: A Journal of Prose Poetics*

Thirteen years ago, I couldn't give away a copy of *The Prose Poem: An International Journal,* and very few books of prose poetry were being published. Those of us who were writing those unpublished books used to share rejection letters, rating them according to levels of stupidity. But things have changed. Last year two first books of prose poems received, respectively, the Walt Whitman Award and the Agnes Lynch Starrett Prize; and three out of the last five James Laughlin Award winners were books that consisted mostly, or exclusively, of prose poems. Nowadays, it's hard to find a book of poetry that doesn't include a prose poem or two. The recent rise of the prose poem is the best and worst thing that has happened to American poetry. The best because poets now feel comfortable moving between prose and verse, the worst because prose poems are multiplying faster than cockroaches, and, in this respect, quantity doesn't equal quality. Maybe this proliferation of prose poetry accounts for why so many poets are disassociating themselves from the genre by inventing more names for what they're writing than my *Book of Slang* has for "penis" and "vagina": microfictions, poetic prose, short-shorts, narratologies, and so on.

This avoidance is not new. W. S. Merwin, in his forward to *Houses and Travelers,* confessed that he didn't know what a prose poem was. He was more interested in "raising some questions about accepted boundaries and definitions." Naomi Shihab Nye, in her chapbook *Mint,* maintained that she wrote "paragraphs," not prose poems; and Robert Hass, concerning the prose in *Human Wishes,* argued that he "never particularly loved the *idea* of the prose poem," with its ties to surrealism, but instead wanted to create a "larger form that might mix verse and prose." More recently, in an interview with *Rain Taxi,* James Tate seems ambivalent about the prose poem, insisting that he "was keeping line breaks" in the poems from *Memoir of the Hawk*— poems reviewed as prose poems, most notably by Charles Simic and Marjorie Perloff. He adds that he "wasn't upset in the least" when I published these poems as prose poems, not explaining why he would submit poems with line breaks to a prose-poem journal, which is like taking your straight son to the father-daughter dance.

Why don't poets want to be associated with the prose poem? For one thing, what decent poet would want to be handcuffed by something as artificial as genre? All poets strive to be original. As Merwin writes, "I realized that I did not want these writings, if they ever came to comprise a substantial group, to qualify for membership in some recognizable genre." But he later admits that "fragments, essays, journal entries, instructions and lists, oral tales and fables" were all precedents for his short prose. Another reason poets have been in denial about prose poetry is because most poets take pride in being subversive, and it's no fun shooting dad the finger if everyone else in the neighborhood is doing it. A poet's worst nightmare is to be fashionable, and the prose poem has certainly become fashionable.

In spite of these denials, the term prose poem works for me, and the current need to escape from it seems doomed. For better or worse, from the moment we began to read fables, fairy tales, parables, fragments, and, even, alas, prose poems, we were somehow contaminated and subject to influences. Actually, the more we try to escape from a genre the more we are entrapped by it, like the child who becomes a carbon copy of the parent by trying too hard not to be. During the first prose-poem renaissance, Michael Benedikt gave his now-famous "working definition" of the prose poem: "It is a genre of poetry, self-consciously written in prose, and characterized by the intense use of virtually all the devices of poetry, which includes the intense use of devices of verse." This description is broad enough to include the surrealist prose poem, the "new sentence," the Emersonian riff, you name it. Certainly, it's worthwhile to explore the gray areas around the prose poem, yet we can sympathize with Tate when, concerning his so-called prose poems, he says, "I'd just as soon not talk about it."

Fortunately, there's nothing too scary about the "sentence," which happens to be the name of this journal. For me, it's a fortuitous name because for once I am not expected to unravel all the complexities of the prose-poem-as-genre. That's Brian Clements' job, and I gladly leave it to him. But, in spite of this editorial get-out-of-jail-free card, for the record, and without further comment, I hereby maintain that the following works are indeed prose poems, except for one which is technically a poetic-prose parable, and another which is a fragment disguised as a memoir which itself is based on a famous fairy tale …

My Ten Favorite Books (At Least for This Week)

Kim Addonizio, *Tell Me*
The Poetry of Catullus, trans. G.H. Sisson
Stephen Dobyns, *Cemetery Nights*
Russell Edson, *The Reason Why the Closet-Man Is Never Sad*
Max Jacob, *The Dice Cup: Selected Prose Poems,* ed. Michael Brownstein
Vladimir Nabokov, *Lolita*
Nicanor Parra, *Antipoems: New and Selected,* ed. David Unger
Charles Simic, *The World Doesn't End*
Bruce Smith, *The Other Lover*
James Tate, *Selected Poems*

Poets always complain about how difficult it is to publish books of poetry, yet hundreds appear every year, and many major poets seem to publish a new book every other year. Why? Partly because publishers will print anything they write; partly because they have jobs with little or no teaching, which frees up a tremendous amount of time. I mean, if you're getting paid a lot of money to teach one or two days a week, you better be writing something. The literary scene is indeed manic, as if whoever publishes the most poems is the best poet. Consequently, most books are thin at best, and if you leaf through the last three books of your favorite poet—books probably published within a four or five year period—you'll realize that if your favorite poet had been patient and chosen the best poems from his last three books, he would have written one of those volumes poets call their "favorite" books—ones they return to over and over again for solace, for inspiration, even for entertainment. Many of my favorite books, ones that continue to influence my own poetry and fiction, are classics such as Ovid's *Amores,* anything by Sappho or Shakespeare, Andreas Capellanus's *The Art of Courtly Love,* Voltaire's *Candide, Don Quixote, Gulliver's Travels,* and Novalis's and Kafka's short prose. But in compiling this list, except for one classical author, I decided to privilege some contemporary books I often reread whenever I'm bored or unable to write. Although I can think of at least ten more books, I'll stick with these for now:

Tell Me: No fluff here. Poem after poem rocks with cruelty and compassion. It's very easy to become self-indulgent or oversentimental when dealing with Addonizio's subject matter. So easy to romanticize and idealize drunks and drug addicts, or to feel sorry for oneself or one's personal history or past mistakes. Yet, with dark irony, Addonizio embraces her own and everyone else's bumps and bruises. "I am going to stop thinking about my losses now," the narrator of the title poem says, "and listen to yours. I'm so sick of dragging them / with me wherever I go, like children up too late / who should be curled in their own beds."

The Poetry of Catullus: Whatever happened to the invective—the fine art of skewering someone? Every night we're assaulted by the unreality of Reality TV, and every morning we're greeted by another stupid war, while our poets unashamedly hawk their poems like insurance salesmen or traveling medicine men. It's certainly time for another Catullus. "Thallus, you pansy, softer than rabbit's wool / The down of a goose or the lobe of an ear, / Softer than an old man's penis and the cobwebs hanging from it / ... Give me back my cloak, you stole it ..." Enough said.

Cemetery Nights: Probably my favorite contemporary book of verse poetry. A making of new myths and a wacky retelling of old ones, played out in a world overseen by a God wearing blinders. Yet amidst the absurdity and horror, optimism and compassion lurk. Consider this from the opening of "Cemetery Nights": "sweet dreams, sweet memories, sweet taste of earth: / here's how the dead pretend they're still alive, / one drags up a chair, a lamp, unwraps / the newspaper from somebody's garbage, / then sits holding the paper up to his face.

/ No matter if the lamp is busted and his eyes / have fallen out...." A contemporary classic.

The Reason Why the Closet-Man Is Never Sad: When I first began writing and submitting prose poems, rejection slips came back, suggesting my poems were cheap imitations of Russell Edson's. Considering I had never heard of Edson, I was a bit shocked, yet believing you should at least read the authors you're influenced by, I bought *The Reason Why the Closet-Man Is Never Sad.* I admire all of Edson's work—its apparent and seductive simplicity, its logical zaniness, its comic-book texture—but this particular book is his best. It's comic, for sure, but also characterized by what he calls the "dark uncomfortable metaphor," suggested by the "closet-man" himself, who tries, hopelessly, of course, to control his life.

The Dice Cup: Selected Prose Poems: Edited and with an Introduction by Michael Brownstein, this is a book I never tire of. Constantly inventive and surprising, Jacob would have made a great stand-up comedian. He does with words what the Cubists did with paint, his greatest virtue being that he never took himself too seriously.

Lolita: How does one make us want to listen to a pedophile go on for over 300 pages? Unreliable narrators are scattered throughout my prose poetry and fiction, and Nabokov's book taught me how to keep them from becoming caricatures. Humbert Humbert sings, and we are seduced by his language while simultaneously questioning his erotic outbursts and lack of self-knowledge. "Lolita, light of my life, fire of my loins. My sin, my soul. Lo-lee-ta: the tip of the tongue taking a trip of three steps down the palate to tap, at three, on the teeth. Lo. Lee. Ta." Whoof!

Antipoems: New and Selected: "Maximum content, minimum words," Parra said. "Economy of language, no metaphors, no literary figures." Funny, angry, self-deprecating, politically savvy, skeptical of grand narratives, all the necessary talents to be a poet in our absurd times. Who else, after years of taunting us, would apologize for his poetry, ask us to burn his book, then say, "I take back everything I said"?

The World Doesn't End: This book of prose poems received a Pulitzer Prize in 1990, much to the dismay of many formalist poets, who were outraged that a book of prose poems could win such a prestigious award. I think it's Simic's best book, and I wish he would write more prose poems. The genre has always welcomed comic juxtapositions and the merging of different genres, making it a fertile place for Simic's prodigious imagination. The simplicity of this book still astounds me.

The Other Lover: A book that was up for a National Book Award the same year as Addonizio's *Tell Me.* All of Smith's talents come together here. Equally adept at formal patterns or the prose poem, he's a troubadour of lost love, a social critic, a blues-and-jazz man, both learned and hip. A very American book, with poems full of loss and love, all held together by wisdom and compassion.

Tate's *Selected Poems:* Constantly surprising, Tate is a comic genius. Marjorie Perloff argued that Rimbaud's "multiplicity of meaning gives way to a strange new literalism." Ditto for Tate. Reading his poems, I often feel as if I'm visiting another planet, governed by a philosopher king wielding a whoopee cushion instead of Excalibur. Tate should be given a Pulitzer Prize for his titles alone: "Same Tits," "Goodtime Jesus," "Teaching the Ape to Write Poems" …

INTERVIEWS

The Art of the Prose Poem: An Interview with Russell Edson

To readers of contemporary American poetry, Russell Edson needs no introduction. This interview took place during many years of correspondence, and went through numerous revisions.

Peter Johnson: What do you think accounts for the recent prose-poem renaissance? So many current collections contain both verse and prose poetry. Even Robert Pinsky's *The Want Bone* has a long prose poem in it. Moreover, there are four recent anthologies, at least five critical studies, and a few journals dedicated to prose poetry, though you still don't see many prose poems in those *The Best of American Poetry* series or in the Pushcart Prizes. And you rarely, if ever, see books of prose poetry winning the thousand or so contests out there.

Russell Edson: Being pretty isolated, what I know of prose poetry comes mostly from your journal. Each issue proves there are an amazing number of people writing them. In some ways, ways of writing are like styles of clothing. Hemlines rise and fall. What's out one year is in the next year. Maybe prose poets are fashion-conscious animals. Other kinds of animals seem to wear the same styles of clothes for centuries and more. Some of us are even monkey-see-monkey-do types. Not to mention that prose poems have that easy-to-write look. But I agree that although there seems to be great interest in the prose poem today, it hasn't gotten the legitimacy of regular or line verse. Which is all to the good from my point of view. Boxes tend to dry up my creativity. The prose poem allows the individual to create his or her own boundaries. It's kind of a naked way to write. And in terms of prizes, I might mention a book of prose poems, Charles Simic's *The World Doesn't End,* which won a Pulitzer a few years back.

PJ: That's a good point, but it's also important to note that Simic's award shook up a few formalists, and I've heard some people suggest that the poetry establishment was willing to "allow" Simic his book of prose poems because he was already an established verse poet, and because he is associated with a certain European sensibility.

RE: The good writer tries to write beyond genre. That hypothetical community you mention means nothing to the real business of writing. And, in the end, the only value any literary award has is its dollar worth, so that one ends up an old man with a mouth black with caviar and eyes red with Bloody Marys. Without a wink from heaven what does human approval mean?

Perhaps you've heard of the Nobel Prize. It's a white-tie affair. The king of Sweden, after handing over the kronur, gives you a swift kick in the ass for luck. He's a large man and, adhering to some old tradition of the Swedish throne, wears horseshoes. I understand it really hurts. He once kicked a recipient to death in front of an international audience:

PJ: So you'd risk a good trouncing for all that cash?

RE: Though a high honor to be kicked by a king wearing horseshoes, it's hardly sweet as a Bloody Mary with a wedge of lime. Still, the risk is well worth it. Probably the worst part of the whole thing is that white-tie getup. I prefer a nightshirt and a sleeping cap. Bedroom slippers are optional. Some like to go to awards ceremonies barefoot, it makes them feel like pilgrims.

PJ: That costume certainly seems like the perfect getup for the prose poet, even though few poets want to embrace the title. Just recently in *Poetry East,* Robert Hass, commenting on a prose piece, made it clear that it really wasn't a prose poem. He called it a "one-paragraph story."

RE: What name one gives or doesn't give to his or her writing is far less important than the work itself. I called my first published book fables, looking, with the help of this label, for a way to describe the pieces I had been writing since sexual awareness. But fables are message stories, and I don't like messages. Fairy tales say in their openings, we're not real, but we're fun. My purpose has always been reality, and it still is.

At that time in my career, the term prose poetry seemed more related to French toast or French fries. I learned to write by writing, but with an intuition for a way that wasn't more than what I could bring to it. Something having no more pretension than a child's primer. Which may be its own pretension. Today the current coinage "prose poem," seems to fit my description without too much fuss. What's in a name ... Or, as Gertrude Stein might say, a rose is a rose is a rose....

PJ: Admittedly, any strict definition of a genre limits its possibilities but your own comments on the fairy tale and fable suggest how taking note of a certain genre's characteristics allows works associated with that genre to speak to each other. For example, you mention Stein. What should we call those prose pieces in *Tender Buttons?* What would they say to Edson's prose poems if they stumbled upon them in the murky passageways between genres?

RE: Stein wrote the way we think, the personifications and the lyric repetition of thought. She becomes the objects in her poems, and they think. You could call the pieces in *Tender Buttons* prose poems. Heck one can call most anything a prose poem. That's what's great about them, anything that's not something else is probably a prose poem. That's why they offer unique ways of making things.

PJ: Okay, but let me harp on this genre issue a bit longer

RE: The word genre, which I also use, makes something in me giggle. But go ahead and harp.

PJ: What I'm saying is that I've come to see that established verse poets don't mind writing prose poems, but they don't want to be closely associated with the genre for fear of not being taken seriously. They treat the prose poem like a one-night stand, something to toy with once in a while, something to dabble in.

RE: What you say is probably true. While most writers hope to do original work, they finally settle into mainstream mediocrity. There is a strong bovine element in most people that watches what the rest of the flock is doing. Everyone wants to succeed one way or another. Still, if one cannot accept failure and scorn, how is he to make his art? It's like wanting to go to heaven without dying. There is too much emphasis on genre vis-à-vis the prose poem. For me the spirit of the prose poem is writing without genre; to go naked with only one's imagination.

PJ: How do you see the sometimes problematic relationship between poetry and prose, which causes so many poets, critics and anthologists anxiety? I've seen your poems in anthologies of "sudden fictions," "micro-fictions," and "modern parables." And yet you consider yourself to be a prose poet.

RE: "Sudden fiction," "micro-fiction," etc. are dodges, and even more artificial sounding than the term *prose poem.* The term prose poem at first glance may seem an oxymoron, until one remembers that the opposite of prose is verse, and that the opposite of poetry is fiction; that verse itself does not a poem make, nor does prose alone a fiction make. In simplified terms, fiction is consciousness language. Poetry is a thing of gesture and sign and almost a non-language art. Poetry and fiction are two sides of the same coin. But neither succeeds without being something of the other. Pure poetry, for instance, is silence. It was fiction that taught poetry how to speak. The personal journey of the prose-poem writer recapitulates this process. It's a primitive pleasure enjoyed by intuitive simpletons.

PJ: Sounds like good distinctions for aspiring simpletons to consider.

RE: The best advice I can give is to ignore advice. Life is just too short to be distracted by the opinions of others. The main thing is to get going with your work however you see it. If you can't do it on your own, it's probably something that's not worth your doing. The beginning writer has only to write to find his art. It's not a matter of talent. We're all talented. Desire and patience take us where we want to go. The world is a strange place, it helps to think of oneself as a secret agent.

PJ: You mentioned earlier that you wanted your poetry to have "no more pretensions than a child's primer," and in "Portrait of a Writer as Fat Man," you disparage the poet who "neglects content for form; thus, in extremity, form becomes content. The ersatz sensibility that crushes the vitality; the how-to poets with their endless discussion of breath and line; the polishing of the jewel until it turns to dust." It's clear that you dislike self-consciousness in poetry, which besides ruining poems, accounts for idiosyncratic theories on poetry or impassioned personal manifestos. "An Historical Breakfast" seems to satirize this self-consciousness and narcissism. And yet how do we poets avoid being self-conscious "with all those yet-to-be-born eyes of the future watching"?

RE: Yes, that's a fun piece, a sketch of a harmless simpleton, encumbered by the yet-to-be-born eyes of the future. But the piece is too silly to have the reality necessary for satire, though it can be taken that way. But on the business of content and form, simply said, an empty poem is like an empty coffin full of nothing but padding. A mental coffin, as it were, without an exquisite corpse or a psychological body. In the first place I write to be entertained. Which means surprised. A good many poets write out of what they call experience. This seems deadened. For me the poem itself, the act of writing it, is the experience, not all the dark crap behind it. To quote Robert Bly, or the Capt. as I like to call him, in his *American Poetry (Wilderness and Domesticity):* "In art, I want to see the 'unknown' looking at me." I want this, too, particularly in my own work.

PJ: And yet, in spite of your insistence on impersonality, I think of you as being one of the most original writers of your generation.

RE: Isolation, like virtue, is its own reward. I like the idea of one's own shop. The idea of the homemade and the simple. Simple is as simple does. It takes a simpleton. I'm the right man for the job. If I've done anything special, and of course I have, it's just by doing what anybody could have if they thought it worth doing. It's understandable that writers want to work with what they consider important themes. I go the other way. I like making something out of almost nothing at all. It leaves room to imagine rather than retelling what one already knows. I think of myself more as an inventor than a decorator.

PJ: Have you always considered yourself to be a loner?

RE: Early on I looked for the company of other writers, "a community of writers to have a conversation with," as you once put it. That's normal and encouraging, but something I never found. Been digging the same hole for years. So it is that Little Mister Prose Poem is currently not doing much thinking that would interest anyone. His ideas haven't changed over the years because there hasn't been anything to change for lack of ideas. There's only the writing, which I admit to knowing very little about. But then it's probably best not to know. It allows one to work without expectation. Best to let the poem do the thinking while we concern ourselves with what's called the personal life.

Unfortunately, poetry now is a social club. One has not only to write well, if one can, but be a social creature. The social part is probably the most important part. And I ain't social. Actually, one doesn't really have to write too well if one is a pleasant person to find a career in writing. But it's not the proper field for a hermit. He would do better cultivating mushrooms in the cave of his thoughts. Communing with bats that live in his personalized belfry.

PJ: But can't an exaggerated isolation—continuous, uninterrupted time with oneself—nurture the kind of self-consciousness you want to avoid?

RE: If self-consciousness is inevitable, as the saying goes, relax and enjoy it. Still, my best pieces seem written by someone or something else. I don't mean "automatic writing," or "stream-of-consciousness," exactly. But writing in such a way that one dreams while being fully awake. Being able to critique (the act of the good editor) as the work begins to form on the page. In a sense, this kind of writing needs to be orderly and compact because it has no set borders. There's only room for working parts. The writer needs the courage to drop "good stuff" for the sake of the poem's psychological movement. Another fault occurs with the writer who doesn't trust his imagination and does too much situating, or scene-setting. The result is too many words chasing too few ideas. Remember, words are the enemy of poetry.

PJ: When you mention "automatic writing" and dream thinking, I can't help thinking of surrealism. You are thought to be a surrealist, but it seems from your comments above that you are making clear distinctions between your process of writing and the way someone like Andre Breton wrote. Every semester I have trouble with a few students who, after reading surrealistic prose poems, defend the random imagery in some of their weaker poems by reminding me of Breton's theory of "automatic writing." They say that I don't understand their poems because I'm not supposed to. They argue that, like the original surrealists, they are writing against rationalism, against logic.

RE: Your students who fall back on Breton's "automatic writing" are under the delusion that anything goes. Well, it doesn't. A piece of writing must not only have the logic of language, but the logic of composition. Automatic writing doesn't begin anyplace, and doesn't end anyplace. It's like a digestive system without a defined mouth or an asshole. A poem is a mental object and requires one's best mental abilities. We work best when our intellects and imaginations are in harmony at the time of the writing. But I like to go real fast before I ruin what I'm writing by thinking about it. This is not automatic writing. It's looking for the shape of thought more than the particulars of the little narrative. But why should we have to be surrealists? Breton didn't invent our imaginations.

PJ: What do you mean by the shape of thought?

RE: It has to do with an abstract argument between reality and the organ of reality (the brain). This means I cannot afford to violate the logic of the prose. My pieces, when they work, though full of odd happenings, win the argument against disorder through the logic of language and a compositional wholeness. So my ideal prose poem is a small, complete work, utterly logical within its own madness. This is different than surrealism, which usually takes the commonplace and makes it strange, and leaves it there.

PJ: And how does dream thinking come into play here?

RE: Dreaming awake, as I've called it, means being fully conscious while tapping into the subconscious or dream mind. This is what any creative writer does. Writers have been doing this for centuries before Breton stumbled upon Freud. Anything that seems a bit odd is labeled surrealism. So many so-called surrealistic poems come across as stylized fakes, as very conscious attempts to be strange. My desire has always been to argue the case for reality. A good example is found in the works of Kafka, who explored the vaunted dreamscape, and yet was able to report it in rational and reasoned language. Language is sanity. We all teeter on the border of dream and consciousness. To pretend insanity is insulting, both to the clinically insane, and to those of us who strive for reality. Dreams, no matter how absurd or strange, are believable because they make physical sense. It's the same creative process as found in poems. The big difference is that dreams are almost totally without language. Still the poem and the dream arise from the same place. It's a place of image and gesture. Which makes the prose poem a miraculous contradiction. Which also makes the writing of the same an act of sanity; whole-brain thinking. Language is a consciousness but the source of the creative is not. It's all a kind of dreaming awake. Again, whole-brain thinking. This is at least what I've come to in my own writing. It really comes down to an intuition more than a technique.

PJ: You certainly sound like a neo-surrealist to me.

RE: Okay, so I'm a neo-surrealist. That's still better than being a neo-fascist. But if I'm anything neo it's not by design; more by blunder and, in the beginning, an unfocussed passion for the arts. One must grant that Breton was right to see the importance of dream thinking. It is the source of the creative energy. l think all people in the arts tap this whether they know it or not; and always have. But, as I mentioned above, there is a dirty little secret about dreams: they are mostly, if not entirely, non-verbal. Dreams create their art works at night in a language of signs, images, gestures and metaphor, all in a dumb show. The subconscious doesn't know how to speak in the conscious language. Trying to put a dream into words is like trying to translate a painting into words. This is the difficulty with poetry.

The poet has to create into language something that has no language. Dreaming awake, as I've called it, means being fully conscious while also dreaming. Not falling asleep on the job, but with a conscious eye to composition; the good editor, as it were. Insanity is always at the elbow, and so I try for order on the page. The insane lose that border between the subconscious and consciousness, and come to frozen laughter. Perhaps that's what the surrealists were looking for as a way of opening a new age.

PJ: All well and good, but what do you say to the student who says, "I love these wacky Edson poems, but what do they mean?"

RE: I don't know exactly. But I don't need to know. As I've said, I am more interested in the shape of thought than the actual thought. The poem thinks well. So the prose poem wants to make some wacky physical sense. It's a matter of simplicity, of being able to think in a physical way. More gesture than word. The hell with reality and meaning. What the writer finds on his page is only the dry, whispery hiss of meaning. This is what makes writing the most human of the arts. One shouldn't have to explain anything to the reader. My approach is to grasp the seemingly irrational and to make something rational of it. To enter sanity by entering sanity's back door. Unless one is describing something entirely different than what one knows of the given world, description is deadly to a prose poem. You were right when you once said that the whole prose poem is the metaphor. The art that laughs at itself with most serious purpose. I never liked the term "experimental writing," but what else is a prose poem? Having written a number of them, I still don't know how they're written.

PJ: Even though it's silly to symbol hunt or search for a one-to-one correspondence in your work, I still see some kind of referentiality at work—in short, some kind of meaning, even in the broadest sense of the word. Consider "The Large Thing"; by following its shape of thought, one of my students suggested it was a comic glance at uncertainty or insatiability, or a parody of that kind of thinking process.

RE: Again the question of satire, and again its possibility. But as I say, I write for amusement, not to change others. I don't know what "The

Large Thing" is, or even what it means. Its movement in and out of the piece has its own reason in logic. I write as a reader, not knowing what the author will say next. The piece is simple and mysterious, as is the soliloquist of the piece, known only as someone. It's really the way I like to write. An abstract something in motion within its own terms. It might be noted how amused infants are by the famous peekaboo game, which starts with the sense of loss, quickly relieved by the return of the mother.

The Capt. goes the other way. He's the soliloquist of his poems. His poems have purpose and are written to do things, such as moral instruction, and beautifully worked nature studies that portray the poet as an alert and sensitive observer of things that many of us might have missed. He is his poems. I, on the other hand, want nothing to do with what I write except the fun of writing it. For me writing is another life lived in another place, an artificial creation organized like a dream.

Charlie Simic speaks to this in his introduction to the prose-poem feature published in a past volume of *Verse,* saying, "Others pray to God. I pray to chance to show me the way out of this prison I call myself." I understand in a very personal way what he means. One sometimes needs a vacation from the idea of oneself. The prose poem is the perfect vacation spot. I've been going there for years.

PJ: Even though it's difficult to think of Bly writing a poem without having a theory about it, he still, especially in his prose poems collected in *What Have I Ever Lost By Dying?,* succeeds in achieving a certain universality. In other words, any theories he has usually do not destroy his overriding impulse to escape from personality into the object. The Language poets also strive for impersonality, and yet I see their work as being very different from yours. I would think they would be more interested in the shape of language than the shape of thought.

RE: Unfortunately I don't know that particular book by Bly. But whatever theories the Capt. comes up with, and he has lots of them, at least they're fun and full of imaginative energy with the worthy enthusiasm of a little boy in a toy shop. This is a far cry from the dour, hardline, so-called Language poets, who are like painters who, instead of painting, spend their days smelling their brushes and easels thinking that a new age is about to dawn.

PJ: And yet many of the poems in *What a Man Can See* (1969) seem to foreshadow the linguistic experiments of Language poetry. Look at a passage from that book:

> A man who said lobster when a basket was in a house, where a child eats an orange to please a ceiling, or dreams and dies.
>
> There was an orange that had a dream in a fruit bowl, the orange dreamed that at the age of puberty life is very good when it is.
>
> The man said lobster when a basket was in a house, but secretly removed by agents of the statue which stood quietly in the square.
>
> The ceiling pleased grew displeased and then grew pleased again.
>
> To have said lobster when a basket is not in a house is to have said lobster when a basket is not in a house, he did not like to say lobster when a basket is not in a house […]
>
> ("There Was")

In this excerpt I see the linguistic play, the non-sequiturs, the reliance on metonymy and synecdoche that I associate with much Language poetry. Two questions: 1) how would you respond to my observations on that book? 2) What made you abandon this kind of experimentation? Because it's clear that in the Russell Edson Canon *What a Man Can See* is a bit of an anomaly.

RE: Metonymy? Synecdoche? You do me too much honor. Actually, that was written many years before its copyright date. I know this will sound strange, but it is possible to do a few things on one's own. Movements bore me. They're usually peopled by those needing umbrellas even when it's not raining; serious little Marxists with their manifestos and their "new" baloney. We all know what the proof of the pudding is, and it's not some overworked political recipe. The main thing is the creative lust, the immediate need to make something. Theory then comes too late. In this sense the completed work becomes the theory of itself. Of course I saw that in the future there would be others trying this road, and hoped that they would see that this kind of writing could only lead to the smelling of brushes and easels, seeking the bitch of meaning, as it were.

PJ: When you did abandon linguistic experimentation after *What a Man Can See,* you seem to lean into a certain recognizable way of writing. We know an Edson poem when we see one. I can think of other writers with equally recognizable styles: Stein and Hemingway, for instance. These styles are easy to parody, and some of the worst of Hemingway and of Stein read like parodies of some of the best of Hemingway and of Stein. I have heard people complain that sometimes your work seems too predictable because you rely on the same simple Dick-and-Jane style. How would you respond to that criticism?

RE: I've read parodies of my work. And often they were as good or even better than what I've done. As I've said, anybody could write like Edson if they wanted to. I find myself doing it all the time. The famous Czech poet, Dr. Miroslav Holub, who is also a medical scientist, says that when he reads Russell Edson he becomes Russell Edson. Of course he understands this is not a good idea. And, from personal experience, I can attest to this. At least Dr. Holub could escape Russell Edson, if he would. I'm trapped, as the Capt. once put it.

This Russell Edson, as part of his baggage, values the articles of speech as the most beautiful arts of the language. He counts three, but there may be more. He's still looking. Though he may favor the indefinite ones, he loves them all, the way they give thingness to the world. He would, if it were possible, write with only these three beautiful words. But without a proper disciplining what can one do with only three words? This is why he's in constant search for other English articles. Of course it's always good fun for a critic to put a writer against himself. It's sort of a I-gotcha-game where the author is squeezed into a small cage of the critic's description, while the critic pokes him through the bars.

I've never seen anything wrong with Dick and Jane. Some might say, well, that's what's wrong with you. I say back, there's nothing wrong with me, albeit nothing right, either, except perhaps my politics. Again this is all part of Russell Edson's baggage. Modernism is the disease of the proclaimed avant-gardes.

PJ: Earlier, you complained about the need of Language poetry to find a theory for itself. Do you think since Pound and Eliot that American poetry, in general, has become too bogged down in theory?

RE: Overweening Poundcake has always seemed to me the rhetorical triumph of personality and mannerism over product. Whatever you might think of Eliot, who has been referred to as Tough-Shit Eliot by those who haven't found his nervous twitterings too attractive, he is the better poet by far, writing some very compelling lyrics to a point.

Theories? This is why it is best to imagine one's skull as a chamber of fetal hair waiting to sprout into a fetching pompadour. Incidentally, the basic recipe for poundcake is a pound of flour, a pound of butter and a pound of sugar....

PJ: You mentioned Bly before. What was it like during the '70s when you, Bly, Tate and others were writing prose poems? Was there a lot of dialogue among you about the form? How did you come to know these people?

RE: Back then, as you probably know, prose poems were illegal. Jim and the Capt. and I had begun to meet secretly, never meeting twice in the same place for fear of the poetry police. It was a heady time, the world had suddenly become new, the heavier-than-air flying machine had just been invented, Eiffel was building a tower made of iron, I forget just where, but everything seemed to be opening at once, even as we were designing what would become the literary future of America. We were all in our teens, which accounts for our belief in the future. We were teenage visionaries.

After long evenings of talking prose poems we'd relax by trying to guess who was ghostwriting all the stuff that was appearing in all the poetry magazines. It looked like the work of a single hack. We never found out. But, like most unsolved murders, the books are still open.

PJ: Were you surprised when Simic's prose poems began appearing in little magazines? His prose poetry in *The World Doesn't End* seems so different from what previously had been published by American prose poets. I know you're friends with Charlie. Did he correspond with you about his sudden prose-poem conversion?

RE: "Prose-poem conversion" sounds a little like a religious event. Well, yes, prose poems look easy precisely because they are. The hardest part for many who would write them is accepting how easy they are to write, and having the courage to write them in spite of that.

Of Charlie's writing prose poems, he contacted me one night telepathically asking my aesthetic blessing. I assured him, telepathically, that is, that he had always had it, and more. I advised him that a telepathic nod from me may not be enough, that he might want to clear it with Jim Tate, to be sure. And thus, *The World Doesn't End.* The book is probably the result of an aesthetic nervous breakdown. So many fine prose poems arise from the need to find poetry again in the way it was originally found. Charlie is an original. There are not too many of us.

PJ: I think of you and Simic as being primarily comic writers. You once wrote that the prose poem that does not have some sense of the funny is flat, and has no more life than a shopping list. First, do you think that the prose poem by its very nature lends itself to humor? Secondly, how would you judge—though I know you won't like that verb—so many books of prose poems that are not comic? I've read very good books of prose poetry that are downright depressing. Have you changed your opinion about the relationship between prose poetry and the comic, considering that the prose poem has evolved so much since 1980 when you made that statement?

RE: Heck, there's nothing wrong with a sad prose poem as long as it's funny. The sense of the funny is the true sense of the tragic. That's what funny is all about. In that the prose poem is a critique of the very act of writing, it's probably so surprised that anybody would be writing it that it almost giggles as it finds itself on the page.

Poetry is very serious business.

PJ: When I speak with you about your work and Simic's and Bly's, I'm reminded of how many poets you all have influenced. Is there any writer who has influenced you?

RE: An influence, if it has any positive meaning, is really a kind of permission that allows us to open something in ourselves. It's there, but we have to learn to recognize it. Then one sees a commercial on TV or reads something in a newspaper or perhaps sees an oddly shaped cloud, and suddenly possibilities begin to be suggested.

I suppose my strongest influence was Russell Edson. Although I never quite understood what he was doing, he was doing something that inspired me to feel it was possible to make things out of almost nothing at all. That's a very creative feeling, starting from almost zero and being able to make something that's at least trivial. And sometimes to make something somewhat more than trivial. But trivial will do. At least it's more than the zero of nothing. People tend to aspire to more than they need, when in the end they turn out to be just another corpse belonging to the general ecology.

PJ: Well, put another way, whom does Edson read when he dons his night shirt, sleeping cap, slippers and parachute, then collapses into his cast-iron La-Z-Boy?

RE: I do as little reading as possible. Reading is a busman's holiday. Of all the arts, literature is probably the least attractive. But, of all the arts, the most human and the most disturbing. I like to read, when I can choose it, scientific materials written for the layman. I like to think about the beginnings, the "big bang," that supposedly erupted from something smaller than an atom. Perhaps from nothing at all. I try to understand it emotionally. My intellect can't handle it.

PJ: Is that why you make fun of physics and astronomy in poems like "The Matter" and "The Dark Side of the Moon." Your prose poetry seems skeptical of mathematical and philosophical formulas that try to make sense of things. I can't see you as a believer in The Great Chain of Being unless you decide to hang an ape from it.

RE: It's just my way of showing fondness. Had I the intellect and the training I should rather have worked in science than anything else

I've done. And I'll not be the first to say that physics is probably the masterpiece of the 20th century. In that piece, "The Dark Side of the Moon," I invented a new sea, which no one has questioned. So in a small way I have added something to the atlas of the moon.

PJ: Finally, I've heard you read twice, and both times I enjoyed your ability to improvise. You had the timing of a stand-up comic. What tip would you give to the poet, especially the comic poet? It's a terrible feeling to read a funny poem to an audience who is expecting to witness the profuse, psychic bleeding of one's heart.

RE: There are probably no cultural events so boring as many poetry readings, due, to no small extent, to the fact that a good many of them present self-serious poets who sing-song odes to their feelings out of their armpits. I can think of nothing so vulgar as watching a confessional poet's guts slowly oozing out of one of his pant legs. But worse than even these abuses are those awful little scene-setting, folksy anecdotes used to shore up meaningless poems.

Nevertheless, for the shy beginner with a bit of pluck there are some simple techniques to focus the good will of an audience. One of the best strategies is to pretend to be hopelessly insane. But if this proves to need more finesse than the beginner can muster, a lisp is another good choice; the idea of someone bravely speaking in public with a pronounced speech defect can be quite touching, particularly to people out for an evening of culture. Even a few properly placed belches punctuated with pretended little pukings into a barf bag can bring an audience to its feet with crescendo approval. But probably the easiest and most affecting way to win an audience is to break into tears at the reading stand. And to weep through the entire reading with your face buried in a handkerchief without having read one piece. I've tried all of the above and more. And yet, oddly enough, I've found that audiences are sometimes grateful for just a straight reading. This needs a little more research.

The main thing to remember is that poetry is very serious stuff....

The Art of the Prose Poem: Interview with Robert Bly

This interview occurred over a two-day period (April 6–7, 1997) at the Associated Writing Program Convention, where Robert Bly was a participant in a session titled, "The State of Prose Poetry: Straddling the Imaginary Line Between Poetry and Prose."

Peter Johnson: Why do you think there is a prose-poem renaissance now?

Robert Bly: Baudelaire wouldn't have been surprised: the prose poem, he thought, would be the primary form of the 20th century. Perhaps Giambattista Vico's calendar of cultural stages, which Joyce liked so much, might help explain the appearance of the prose poem. Vico in 1744 laid out three stages of culture, moving from the Gods to the Heroes to Ordinary People—from the Sacred Culture, as in Egypt, to the Aristocratic Culture, as in the Renaissance, to the Democratic. In the Sacred Phase, all words are signs, and the natural form is a sacred chant. In high Greece and Renaissance England, Kings, Queens, heroic types, the class system, metrical poetry, and complicated syntax are the rule. In the third phase, the horizontal phase, meter, syntax, classes, all go; and the natural form is prose.

So we are all secretly longing for prose, which is the natural speech of democratic language, and what Vico calls "epistolatory or vulgar, which serves the common use of life." If one tries to live in one's own age, it doesn't mean abandoning poetry: the task is to keep the mystery, the high spirits, the subtlety, even the verbal brilliance of the two earlier phases, while letting the sentence itself—not the foot or the line—be the primary unit.

Language in the heroic phase moves steadily upward. When Shakespeare creates Bottom in *A Midsummer Night's Dream,* he has already sensed that things have changed. We are in the democratic realm now, and in that realm everything is horizontal and grammar tends to decline into simple sentences. It was William Carlos Williams who tried to face these demands, not Henry James.

PJ: When you mention the "thing-poem" in your essay, "The Prose Poem as an Evolving Form," are you referring to just "object poems," or would your "thing-poems" include such ones as "A Caterpillar" and "An Octopus"?

RB: Oh, certainly. It's inclusive. All creatures like to be looked at.

PJ: Specifically, you say that "in the object poem in prose, the conscious mind gives up, at least to a degree, the adversary position it usually adopts toward the unconscious, and a certain harmony between the two takes place." By "adversary position," do you mean a poet's conscious attempt to manhandle or control the object?

RB: Yes. The mind is always tempted to take up a superior position in relation to beings—such as caterpillars or clams—who are without reason. Many philosophers and saints in the West have made efforts to dissolve the adversarial position human beings take toward animals— St. Francis would be one. It's been slow work.

We could say that in a prose poem one can practice writing about an animal or "thing" in a way that wouldn't be hierarchical, in which one wouldn't place human beings on top and animals on the bottom. I like the way Frost implies in "Two Look at Two" a mysterious sympathy between a human couple and a deer couple. We can feel the lack of hierarchy in Thoreau's prose as well. So what one ultimately hopes for is a lessening of the empire mentality of the human being, shall we say, a disappearance completely of the thought of inferior races and superior races, a giving up completely of the idea that nature has no consciousness. When some adversarial thinking is cleared away, it's possible for language to become transparent. For example, when you read one of Ponge's prose poems, the text, in some way, almost becomes transparent, and one feels one can touch the object itself. That doesn't mean that the prose-poem writer is doomed to be simpleminded. Ponge is the opposite of simpleminded and he has the whole flexibility of the French language at his disposal. Animals, as we know, are very subtle, as are gardens, as are forests. So we need a language with tremendous subtlety, and many shadings. This is how Ponge does his poem on the dinner plate or *assiette*.

> During our consecration here let's be careful not to make this thing that we use every day too pearly. No poetic leap, no matter how brilliant, can speak in a sufficiently flat way about the lowly interval that porcelain occupies between pure spirit and appetite.
>
> Not without some humor, alas, (it fits its animal better), the name for its lovely matter was taken from a mollusc shell. And we, a gypsy species, are not to take a seat there. Its substance has been named porcelain, from the Latin—by analogy—*porcelana*.... Is that good enough for your appetite?
>
> But all beauty, which suddenly rises from the restlessness of the waves, has its true place on a seashell.... Is that too much for pure spirit?
>
> And the assiette, whatever you say, rose in a similar way from the sea, and what's more was multiplied instantly by that free-spirited juggler in the wings who takes the place sometimes of the melancholic old man who tosses us with poor grace one sun per day.
>
> That is why you see the assiette here in its numerous incarnations still vibrating as a skipped stone settles at last on the sacred surface of the tablecloth.
>
> Here you have all that one can say about an object which contributes more for living than it offers for reflection.
>
> (translated by Robert Bly)

PJ: Although I see how your sensibility can be linked to Ponge's, it seems, at times, especially in his later work, that much of his language is scientific, which, to me, implies reliance upon the intellect, and wouldn't you agree that too much intellect tends to distance one from the object? Doesn't the intellect want to "figure out" the object, control it, which seems to be precisely what you're against?

RB: Ponge is a Frenchman! He's not a good example of a poet writing out of the unconscious because he didn't believe in the unconscious! I was amazed when I found that out. He offers the French dictionary instead of the unconscious! We could say that when he wants to escape reason, he turns to the dictionary because it carefully preserves the ancient, biological, mysterious history of every word. By following the tracks left by a word, we can go backward in time. Freud used a dream for that, but Ponge with his intellect is just as clever.

PJ: If Ponge approaches objects through his intellect, do you think that you connect with them more through metaphor, because so many of your thing-poems are loaded with metaphors, some of which even cluster? But it's curious that just as the intellect can manhandle an object, which we might say is not healthy, one can also manipulate it through metaphor. It's a more subtle means of control, but metaphor still implies a certain domination. And so the self has contaminated the union of object and poet, and again that seems to be something you are against, though you have changed your mind lately. I'm thinking of your preface to *What Have I Ever Lost by Dying?* You write, "When I composed the first of these poems ... I had hoped that a writer could describe an object or a creature without claiming it, without immersing it like a negative in his developing tank of disappointment and desire. I no longer think that is possible."

RB: You are afraid that the self will contaminate the union of object and poet? You are right, it will. But so what? When I first began writing poems about box turtles or the feet of wrens, I wanted to be pure: I wanted to have the description free of my Americanness or my sadness. I wanted their colors in the poem, not mine. But if colors don't come in from my psyche, there won't be any colors. There'll only be a negative.

I finally decided that one's task is not only to snap the picture, but to develop it in a dark room. I finally agreed it is all right to claim the creature in some way, by "immersing it like a negative in our developing tank of disappointment and desire."

I said in the introduction you mention: "Our desires and

disappointments have such hunger that they pull each sturgeon or hollow tree into themselves."

How can a poem on an octopus be free of that? No, no! It is impossible! For example, I began a poem on an orange this way: "The orange's hide is soft and grainy, and it has two navels" ... that is the near-sighted, scientific part ... "as if it were born once into this world and once into the next." That last clause is where the life comes in! One half of a metaphor is contributed by the left brain, it's cool and realistic; then the loyal old right lobe, unembittered by its owner's officialized neglect, leaps forward with a suggestion in its own language—an image. The left side grabs it with relief, and out it comes as a metaphor. That is Ted Hughes talking. The curious result is always the same: everybody laughs or at least smiles, or at least feels a sudden lift, a sudden waft of oxygen.

PJ: Your metaphors and similes are odd in that they seem easily apprehended, but as I look closely at them, they become more elusive. I sense a real playfulness in them.

RB: Well, give me an example.

PJ: In "A Box Turtle," you write, "The claws—five on the front, four in back—are curiously long and elegant, cold, curved, pale, like a lieutenant's sword." And in "The Starfish" you describe its arms as being "rolled up now, lazily, like a puppy on its back. One arm is especially active and curves up over its own body as if a dinosaur were looking behind him." [Bly laughs.] Yes, it's comic. And even though there is a visual element to both of these similes, they really defy explication.

RB: How did you feel about the similes in "The Starfish"?

PJ: It goes back to what you said about metaphor reflecting your internal state. Obviously, there is nothing ominous about your starfish. It possesses a sense of wonder and connectedness.

RB: I noticed that the starfish's various arms were doing different things: "many of its arms are rolled up now, lazily, like..., " and the moment you say "like" ... the whole unknown world enters in, and you don't know what you're going to say. At that moment, as Bill

Stafford says, you have to give up all plans and all hope for perfection. Be a good host; let whatever comes in come in. One arm is rolled back a little "like a puppy on its back." I remember writing that and thinking, "Whoa, that's wonderful." A scientist will say," Some of its arms are in a rolled up position." Period. The eye has done that. But I added "lazily," and all of a sudden, something comes in from the part of me that likes lazy people, maybe. And then I say "like" ... and now one is really in the soup. Writing, one has to be playful enough to say, "I'll probably make a fool of myself in this image." Then you can call on the part of yourself that isn't precise, but has seen hundreds of these events when you were ten or twelve or fifteen. You don't know from what era or stage or moment of your life the image is going to come. Had I been feeling reptilian, I might have compared the starfish's curved arm to a snake. In any case, I love that moment when one asks, "Like what?"

Then I wrote, "How slowly and evenly it moves." I'm simply watching the starfish move. But moving like what? I could say it's moving like a racing car stuck in first, or like a snail. But when I say, "The starfish is a glacier," then I'm far ahead, and I have time to make a joke, saying it goes "sixty miles a year"; actually most glaciers go only a foot or two. I go on to say that the starfish is "about the size of ..." what? A "pail." Sometimes when I'm writing I'll put down six nouns at that point: it's the size of a fist, of a dinner plate that's been thrown out into the dump, of a hubcap on a Volkswagen, the lid of a can found underneath the water, or the bottom of a pail. "The bottom of a pail" interests me, because all at once we have a pail; moreover, we have the interesting volume at the bottom of a pail, and perhaps some shady light.

PJ: Well, certain images have more resonances than others.

RB: Yes, and the making of them is so much fun.

PJ: Being an editor of a prose-poem journal, I read work from many poets who try to imitate the Robert Bly thing-poem, and I'm sure they're having fun, too, but somehow they just can't make the leaps you make, whether those leaps come through metaphor or juxtaposition of imagery. I think a certain astonishment is missing in many object poems I receive. For example, I published your poem "An Oyster Shell." Listen to what happens in the first paragraph: "The shell is scarred, as if it were a rushing river bottom, scratched by great trees being carried down. Sometimes its whitish calcium has been folded over itself, as when molten rock flows out; so something is still angry." [Bly laughs.]

So you see what I mean? In your best thing-poems you constantly redirect the reader and reveal strange new associations. I've come to see the object poem as being similar to the still life in painting. Every once in a while I come across an astonishing still life, say by the Irish impressionist O'Connor, but, for the most part, many of them leave me empty. Similarly, many of the object poems I receive remind me of a still life without the banana, devoid of any correspondences, any kind of creative, erotic energy.

RB: My leaps have to do with a confidence that psychology gives me that one can see the invisible. If you glance at a human being and you see the layers of calcium on his face, you are looking at some anger underneath that. That's where the sally in "An Oyster Shell" came from. The fun lies in making unjustified leaps about people and things.

PJ: Yes, and, in this sense, not all your leaps are playful. Very often you deal with what Edson calls "the dark uncomfortable metaphor."

RB: Let's talk about that in a different way. What is the proper subject for a prose poem? There is no answer for that, so you have to look at your own life. I lived my childhood relaxed and on a farm, so when I'm with a tree, I feel relaxed. But a friend of mine who's lived in Manhattan his whole life went for a weekend up to Rye, and when he came back, he said, "Why don't those trees ever say anything?" He'd be better off writing a prose poem in the city, because he feels safe there. Once at a prose-poem workshop in the Village, I asked the students to find some object to write about that was not made by human beings. One poet refused and said: "I'm not going to do that. I don't care beans about pine cones. Instead I'll find you a city object to write about!" He came back after lunch with a small bottle cap entirely full of that grungy dirt peculiar to vacant lots; three long white hairs rose out of it. He wrote about that for hours. His message was, "Throw away pine cones. Get a bottle cap."

PJ: It does seem that you are stuck, or blessed, with the geography of your childhood.

RB: All you have to do is relax into that. Do you remember that little poem David Ignatow wrote about the city? He was asking a wall to bless him. It didn't:

> The wall is silent
> I speak for it,
> blessing myself.

He once dedicated a poem to me, complaining about my constant mentioning of leaves falling: "I wish I understood the beauty / in leaves falling. To whom / are we beautiful / as we go?" That's great, great.

PJ: To change the subject a bit, I'm curious what you think of the prose poem that comes out of what we generally call the "Language school" of poetry.

RB: How would you describe that school?

PJ: I'm thinking of that essay by Ron Silliman called "The New Sentence," and of other comments that he's made. He wouldn't consider the New Prose Poem to be like the prose poetry of French Symbolism, yet I know from editing my journal that many poets associated with that school consider their prose pieces to be prose poems. It's hard to do justice to the Language movement in a few words, but I suppose I'm referring to Silliman's interest in "what a poem is actually made of—not images, not voices, not characters or plots, all of which appear on the paper, or in one's mouth, only through the invocation of a specific medium, language itself." It seems to me that your reliance on metaphor, and your debt to such symbolists as Baudelaire, who himself was such a believer in natural correspondences, would make you someone who writes in a very different way from the Language poets.

RB: What do you make of all this theorizing?

PJ: Some very good work has come out of Language poetry, especially such books as *Lawn of Excluded Middle* and *The Reproduction of Profiles* by Rosmarie Waldrop, but in general, I find most of it too intellectual. I have this feeling that when the Language poets go on vacation, they leave Stein and Wittgenstein at home and take Sappho and Bachelard.

RB: Ha! It seems to me that a lot of them were sorry that they were born into a messy universe, and they'd like to clean it up. It is a messy universe, and metaphors are part of the mess.

PJ: What do you think of Gertrude Stein's work? In many ways, she is the mother of the Language movement.

RB: [a very long pause] I'd like to have more intelligence in a poem. It's as if she's cut off her own legs.

PJ: Could you elaborate on that?

RB: No. There's something amputated there, and to me that's very sad.

PJ: It surprised me in our session this afternoon when you said that in the future the prose poem will become more and more concerned with sound. I have always thought that your primary focus was on the image, without much regard for meter, rhyme, and so on.

RB: Then I should make myself clear.

PJ: But just let me add one more question to the one above. Someone once said to me that when the literary dust settles it will be interesting to see what women and men emerge as the most important influences in twentieth-century American poetry. He suggested that the two most important male figures will be Ezra Pound and you. And then he added with a smile, "Too bad Bly has a tin ear." What do you think he meant by that?

RB: I don't mind people saying those things about me. I say a lot of things about me as well. But let's go back. You are right that I thought at one time the most important task was to bring the image and the metaphor out from its mousetrap of elaborate syntax and meter. It's like rescuing something alive from a burning building. Like rescuing a baby from an orphan asylum. It's a Taoist adventure to save the one detail that has power and imagery in itself. You know when Bashō was walking on that well-known road to the north in Japan, he arrived at a mountaintop which had mainly stones and a lot of tremendous winds. Many poets had written a poem there. Bashō wrote: "Storm on Mount Asama! / Wind blowing out of the stones!" Whoa! I couldn't believe he wrote that! He was able to take the energy of the wind and the energy of the stones and protect them from syntax, protect them from ordinary ideas. I spent a lot of time years ago trying to free the image from its matrix of what I would now call the hierarchical, aristocratic realm.

But then when I got the image in my own work out, I began to say to myself: "This image resonates in the body but not in the ear." And I began to brood over those old sonnets where the sounds resonate and reverberate so marvelously. They repeat but remain entangled. To me the next step was how to bring the sound out from the burning building.

PJ: Do you think this heightened interest in sound explains why you're writing mostly verse poetry now?

RB: Yes. Let's look at this one from *Morning Poems*:

> It's good to stay in bed a while, and hear
> The *ay* slyly hidden in sequacious,
> Scent in summer world the two *ers*
> Listen for the *in* hidden in woodbins.
>
> Am I like the hog snuffling for truffles,
> Followed by skimpy lords in oversized furs?
> For this gaiety do I need forgiveness?
> Does the lark need forgiveness for its blue eggs?
>
> So it's a bird-like thing, then, this hiding
> And warming of sounds. They are the little low
> Heavens in the nest; now my chest feathers
> Widen, now I'm an old hen, now I am satisfied.

Here my aim is to brood over and lift both image and sound away from the matrix of iambic meter. If I can go back to verse with the playfulness I've learned from the prose poem, then I have two forms of playfulness: one with the image and metaphor, and another with the repetition of sound.

PJ: And you think that's harder to do with the prose poem?

RB: No, I don't. I've done a lot of sound-work—repetition of sounds—in prose poems, though few commentators notice it. We can talk about a specific prose poem if you wish.

PJ: I'm all ears.

RB: I've tried in prose poems to lift the sounds up, so to speak. I call sounds such as *er* and *in* and *or* "sound particles." A typical prose poem may use 45 or 70 different sound particles. But if you're going to get musical chimes going, you're better off using as few of these particles as possible and calling them in over and over again. Here's a short prose poem called "A Hollow Tree," probably from 1974.

> I bend over an old hollow cottonwood stump, still standing, waist high, and look inside. Early spring. Its Siamese temple walls are all brown and ancient. The walls have been worked on by the intricate ones. Inside the hollow walls there is privacy and secrecy, dim light. And yet some creature has died there.
>
> On the temple floor feathers, gray feathers, many of them with a fluted white tip. Many feathers. In the silence many feathers.

In "I bend over an old hollow cottonwood stump," we can hear three *oh*'s in a short space. "I bend over an old hollow cottonwood stump, still standing, waist high." Can you hear how the *ay* comes in strongly? And with "high," the first *ai* sound establishes itself, returning again with "inside" and "Siamese." "Early spring. Its Siamese temple walls ..." If you listen to the *ai* in "Siamese," you can see it's very insistent for reasons that are not clear. Now the *awl* sound comes in three times. When one says "the temple walls are all brown and ancient," the *ay* comes in once more, and the *ow* sound becomes linked with *n*'s. And soon the *n* sounds begin to flood the poem with their *n* energy. "The temple walls are all brown and ancient. The walls have been worked on by the intricate ones. Inside the hollow walls ..." We get "been" and "on," "intricate," "ones," and "inside." So that's fun. Now the *ai* sound returns because that sound is about to take over the poem.

"Inside the hollow walls there is privacy and secrecy, dim light. And yet some creature has died here." In some sense, because *ai*'s are coming along, "privacy" itself is identified as an important word. And so it's the *ai* sound that is really doing the emotional work here; and it comes again with "died." In the next paragraph the word "temple" picks up the *m* sound from "stump" and the *m* in Siamese and adds "many." And *f* becomes important. "On the temple floor feathers, gray feathers, many of them with a fluted white tip. Many feathers. In the silence many feathers."

PJ: So much for the lack of thematically linked sounds in your poems.

RB: Ha! You see it's a magical thing.

PJ: I find it hard to believe that you're thinking about all of this when you're writing. Do you think the sound is coming from the object and is not artificially imposed? Or does it come from some natural rhythm in you? I can't believe you had this all figured out before you wrote the poem.

RB: Well, certainly; but your word "before" suggests that the poem was written in one sitting. I must have written at least twenty versions of this poem. And when I began to see that the *ai*'s were becoming colorful, I rewrote the lines in order to add shading to that sound. I think you're right to say that the sounds suggest themselves first in a perfectly natural way. And if you're terribly lucky, the improvisational inspiration will last for the whole poem. Improvisational success usually lasts for only four or five lines. After that you have to say, "Okay, I'm committed to these sounds," and then you have to look at the hundreds of possibilities before you.

PJ: There are some wonderful sounds in your prose poem "Warning to the Reader." That poem seems to me to be your *ars poetica*. The poem is a warning to readers and to writers, and it works so well because of its shifts in thought, especially the huge transition signaled by "But" in the second paragraph. I also think it's one of your darker and more ironic poems. What do you have to say about this prose poem?

Warning to the Reader

> Sometimes farm granaries become especially beautiful when all the oats or wheat are gone, and the wind has swept the rough floor clean. Standing inside, we see around us, coming in through the cracks between shrunken wallboards, bands or strips of sunlight. So in a poem about imprisonment, one sees a little light.
> But how many birds have died trapped in these granaries.
> The bird, seeing the bands of light, flutters up the walls and falls back again and again. The way out is where the rats enter and leave; but the rat's hole is low to the floor. Writers, be careful then by showing the sunlight on the walls not to promise the anxious and panicky blackbirds a way out.
> I say to the reader, beware. Readers who love poems of light may sit hunched in the corner with nothing in their gizzards for four days, light failing, the eyes glazed.... They may end as a mound of feathers and a skull on the open boardwood floor....

RB: Well, the thought or drive of the poem is clear. I say I feel some responsibility through the years for urging readers to look upward, follow Kabir upward. I love ascents—who doesn't love ascents? But still, the old tradition was, no step upward without a step down. No food for the angel without some food for the rat. In "Snowy Fields" I say, "The leaves at the crown of the tree are asleep / Like the dark bits of earth at its root." But the main feeling in "Snowy Fields" is "the joy of sailing and the open sea!" The great joy is to follow the route of Kabir upward to that warm union he so marvelously evokes. Freud is a rat person. Freud is not popular now. It's painful to know how imprisoned our parents and grandparents were—how they couldn't see either the cracks in the walls, nor the rats' holes. With "a mound of feathers" I'm thinking of many unlucky friends in the ashrams.

If we turn and look at the sound now, I can remember writing and rewriting this poem, and deciding very early on the *n* sounds. "Sometimes farm granaries become especially beautiful when all the oats or wheat are gone...." One can say "after the oats or wheat are gone," or "after the oats are hauled away." I had hundreds of possibilities, and settling on *n* helped narrow them down.

PJ: Don't you think those word choices are not really choices, that the right words often just arrive? Is it really such a conscious process?

RB: It wasn't so much a word, it was a sound. "... and the wind has swept the rough floor clean. Standing inside, we see around us, coming in through the cracks between shrunken wallboards, bands or strips of sunlight. So in a poem about imprisonment, one sees a little light." I remember having eight or nine possibilities for the adjective for "wallboards." Wallboards are boards that have been in the sun too long, and they actually become warped and smaller. So we understand there are always dozens of possibilities; but because of the *n*'s, I chose shrunken. The last sentence "So in a poem about imprisonment, one sees a little light" came in during about the fifteenth rewrite.

PJ: I think that sentence is the core of the poem.

RB: Yes. I'm declaring that this poem is not really about nature or farm granaries. "How many birds have died trapped in granaries" that are workshops or meditation retreats that seem to offer life all the time, seem to offer constant glimpses of the spirit. "The bird, seeing the bands of light, flutters up the walls and falls back again and again."

PJ: And then we encounter another big shift.

RB: Yes. As I've said, there's a problem in all this fluttering toward the light, because the "way out" is really where the "rats leave and enter." Baudelaire was a rat. Remember his *Flowers of Evil*. "But the rat's hole is low to the floor." We're citizens of such a great country, why should we bend and go through a rat's hole? "Writers be careful then by showing the sunlight on the walls not to promise the anxious and panicky blackbirds a way out."

Then I decided to repeat the warning: "I say to the reader, beware. Readers who love poems of light may sit hunched," and I'm coming back to the *n*'s, "in the corner with nothing in their gizzards for four days, light failing, the eyes glazed.... They may end as a mound of feathers and a skull on the open boardwood floor...." Some academic poets too "sit hunched in the corner with nothing in their gizzards for four days, light failing, the eyes glazed." I'm not mocking academic poets; I'm saying it is difficult to have to teach ascensionist literature day after day. Ministers and priests suffer from it. So do I. So I had to finish the theme as best I could, but I also had to finish the poem musically with the *n*'s in the last sentence because that's where I began.

PJ: I've also thought how curious that last line echoes the end of "August Rain": "These objects lie against the ship's side, and will nudge the hole that lets the water in at last." Which in that poem is a good thing.

RB: I'm glad you remembered that.

PJ: I have one more question. I always thought that Norman Mailer had the chance to become the greatest American male novelist since Faulkner, but then he became a public figure and I think he lost his focus. To say you've become a public figure would be an understatement. You once said that in the Sixties people were looking for a "hero," and you gladly embraced that role. Well, now you are a hero to some people, but is that good? When you sit down to write, how do you keep from becoming self-conscious? Does the public Robert Bly look over the shoulder of the private-poet Robert Bly? How do you return to that childlike state that you say informs all your poetry? You must know that your many "audiences," whether they come to you through *Iron John* or through *Morning Poems,* have certain expectations. In short, how do you avoid that kind of self-consciousness that will surely destroy any poetic venture?

RB: I don't know what to say about it.

PJ: Have you ever thought you were losing touch with that honest part of you which allows you to write?

RB: No. My wife and I happened to walk past one of those storefront mediums on Sixth Avenue one day. I said, "Let's go." She said, "You go." The medium laid out her Tarot cards and said: "Do you realize that you can be in a room with a hundred people who like you, and you don't even know it?" My wife said, "That's right, that's what he's like." Maybe it's a blessing.

But I'll give you another answer. In your question you wonder whether a successful person may find that some image of himself or herself may interfere with the ability to reach over and touch a rock or an animal or a feeling. Is that right?

PJ: Yes.

RB: But there are hundreds and thousands of people—and I'm one of them—who have an image of themselves as unsuccessful, inadequate, unloved, wrong. And that image of oneself is probably more dangerous than the image of oneself as a famous person.

Let's look at it this way. For most of us, the old, close-knit community has disappeared. A person tended to live inside a group of thirty or forty people who admired him or her because of her character, or intelligence or humor. Emily Dickinson lived in such a community in Amherst. Now we seem to be adrift in what George W. S. Trow calls either "a grid of 200 million" or a grid of one. We want to have love coming from 200 million, because the love of thirty people no longer sustains us.

PJ: That's what I meant at our session yesterday—that for many poets, their fifteen minutes of fame isn't long enough. They want twenty or thirty, or as many as they can get. They're insatiable.

RB: Those are the poets who pester you as an editor, and send fifty poems in one submission. This is a very strange turn of events, and no one knows what will happen next. The longing for fame has virtually destroyed the art world in New York because people don't want to be good artists, they want to be famous. Most artists want a huge exhibition when they're twenty-four. Years ago, most artists would have waited and survived for twenty years on the admiration of their friends, or family, or mentors. I suppose I'm an example—I published my first book when I was 36.

PJ: They don't want to serve an apprenticeship.

RB: A twenty-year apprenticeship may be essential. We remember the

19th-century artist in the garret who wouldn't ask for a grant because he thought that one part of his task as an artist was to be in the garret. I want to suggest that this image that so many artists have of themselves being unloved is more destructive of creativity than the feeling that one is admired. Sometimes I have both feelings at the same time.

PJ: But you must know that you couldn't take a walk downstairs right now without having admirers, some genuine, some sycophants, crowding around you.

RB: But that's the point. How do you know that they're not doing that for some other reason? Maybe the person with taste walked away the minute they saw me coming. But why argue? Both sides of us are pests: the side that feels unloved, and the side that feels admired. I write poems in bed every morning, and, for some reason, when I write like this I feel safe from both of these pests. As Bill Stafford said, during that moment when you're lying there, lying in bed, the only issues are between you and your mind, between you and your soul, and between you and the images coming toward you, whether you're going to welcome them or not. At that moment, you're back to being sixteen years old again. You've never written a poem before; and besides, whatever you have written previously is not going to help you in this particular poem. And if a hippopotamus with a funny laugh and a big green ass comes along, are you going to bring him into the poem or not? From this point of view, it doesn't matter whether you're famous. When you're standing near a hollow tree, the poem lies in the resemblance between you and that hollow tree. You have to deal with the bond between you and the hollow tree. What birds have died inside me hmm? It's almost a gesture of love. So when you're in that state, it doesn't matter if anyone likes you, or even knows who you are.

Interview with Peter Johnson by Steve Frech

Stephen Frech: Jokes and humor have long held a place in psychoanalytic thought, but I read an article by Louis Franzini titled "Humor in Therapy" promoting "formal humor training for therapists." It seems to me that a quality about humor (just like psychology itself) eludes analysis and formal training. Nevertheless, given the humor in your poems, what coping, cathartic, or revelatory qualities do you think humor adds to poems in general or to your poems more specifically? Is humor something that helps you write, then becomes part of the very fabric of the poem?

Peter Johnson: It's a curious idea: therapists learning how to be funny so they can teach others to be funny. If the purpose of this training is to make people laugh at themselves, I'm all for it. Jonathan Swift compares satire to a mirror in which everyone sees everyone's face but their own, which is why they laugh so hard. But in the perfect satire—if we think of satire as actually being able to affect change—we should see our own reflections, and the best satirists are those who realize they possess the traits they satirize. Satire doesn't work when we sense the presence of a smug author looking down at his sniveling creations.

But you're right to stress comedy in my work. I wrote a dissertation on black humor, and my first prose poems were influenced by the ancient Greek writer Theophrastus, who wrote a book of comic character sketches called *Characters*. But if humor has become part of the very "fabric" of my poetry, as you say, that's occurred simply because I view the world comically. I'm a wise guy. I didn't have to invent that persona, so the mixture of the high and low in my work, which creates the humor, is really not deliberate.

SF: So where do you think that comic edge originated for you?

PJ: I grew up in a working-class environment. My father was a mailman and a steel worker, but because I was fairly intelligent and a good athlete, I received a classical education at a Jesuit high school. I spent my formative years straddling high and low cultures, so, in *Miracles & Mortifications,* it comes naturally for me to present Socrates with a booger in his nose or to have Kepler chirping, "Be good to my bird" as he tries "to shake the celestial cacophony from his head." The narrators of the two sections of *Miracles* are funny to watch precisely because they try to embrace grand narratives of high culture while everything is collapsing around them.

In the first section, "Travels with Gigi," the narrator keeps waiting for his girlfriend to behave according to an easily recognizable courtly love tradition, but she's not interested in that tradition; she's unpredictable, a real ballbuster. And in the second section, "Travels with Oedipus," the father needs to believe in a dignified Western historical tradition, while his teenage son just wants to have a good time. My "high," idealistic sensibility sympathizes with the father; my "low," wise-guy sensibility with Gigi and the son. It's the tension between these two that creates most of the humor. It's important to remember that every satirist is really an idealist. You don't obsessively attack or make fun of something unless you're very hurt because that "something" is not living up to your expectations.

Because of my comic sensibility, it makes sense that I rejected all the trappings of verse poetry and turned to the prose poem. Originally, I wanted my poetry to echo the metrical schemes and elevated subjects of those Latin and Greek writers I had translated in high school and college, but the results were always strained, inauthentic. I had the same results with free verse. Though I can't prove it, I think the prose poem wants to be funny.

SF: And the high and low collide from the beginning in your first book. The first time I read the title, *Pretty Happy!,* I laughed out loud: to proclaim one's happiness, but qualify it as only moderate seems a funny mitigating exclamation.

PJ: I'm glad you saw the irony in the title. Irony, of course, is one way into humor. I've always been interested in those ancient comic characters like the eiron (the self-deprecator), the alazon (the impostor) and the buffoon, and those characters are scattered throughout *Pretty Happy!* Very often the humor in those poems occurs when we look at characters differently than they see themselves. Many of my first-person narrators are glass half-empty people, even the narrators who resemble me.

Early in my career, I pictured myself writing and reciting deeply metaphysical poems while being surrounded by fifteen naked Joni Mitchell look-alikes playing recorders fashioned from ivory tusks. But now I embrace anger and even enjoy playing the fool, realizing it suits my temperament. But it's a precarious persona, because it's so easy to become topical or trivial.

SF: In what way is the prose poem, with its inherent confounding genre tension, the exact vessel for the absurd or dark ironic moments you describe?

PJ: As I said, I think it has a predisposition toward comedy. I also wonder if so many prose poets are comic poets because they became interested in the form while reading the French symbolists and surrealists. We can see the beginnings of comic and absurd juxtapositions and puns associated with surrealism, Dada and cubism in the works of Baudelaire and Rimbaud.

SF: I'm very interested in your inclusion of the surrealists and wonder if we could linger there for a moment. Surrealists of all disciplines used conscious strategies (games, optical illusions, juxtapositions) as vehicles for accessing altered or other states of consciousness. Again, perhaps in prose poetry's play of cross genre, we see the irony of conscious access to the unconscious. What can you say about the prose poem as a discourse or even a struggle between the conscious and the unconscious?

PJ: I think the freedom that prose allows encourages the kind of leaping Bly speaks of in his essay "Looking for Dragon Smoke"—a leaping from the conscious mind to the unconscious and back again.

But it's impossible to describe this process; it's intuitive. If we could pinpoint the leaps between the conscious and unconscious in a poem, then it would be a lousy poem. But, still, both parts of the mind must be at work. When I write a poem I bring experiences, emotions—whatever—to it. I trust my imagination to create a poem from this raw material, and in the first draft, I often feel like someone working on a jigsaw puzzle, blindfolded. I guess you could argue that I tap the unconscious here; I guess you could say, as Bly does, that in the prose poem "the conscious mind, at least to a degree, gives up the adversarial position it usually adopts toward the unconscious, and a certain harmony between the two takes place."

But I'm skeptical of saying too much about it. I'm really more interested in another part of the process—the constant rewriting and reinventing every time I go back to the poem. Houdini thought genius was repetition. At times, even he was surprised by some of his escapes, but he believed he reached this mystical state (though he wouldn't have called it that) by repeating his routines over and over, not by invoking the gods. He was referring, I think, to a kind of obsessiveness that is very creative, a kind of controlled pursuit of the G-spot of the poem. If one suffers this process over and over again, it's easier to get there the next time. But, again, you can analyze things too much. When the first volume of my journal came out, someone said that the black-and-white cover captured the poetry-prose and conscious-unconscious oppositions in the prose poem. In fact, the cover was black and white because I started with a $2000 budget and couldn't afford a four-color cover.

SF: Art commentary frequently makes such silly gaffes. Confronted with a sexual reading of his *Upright Motive #5,* Henry Moore says simply that he called the sculpture *The Hole and the Lump* because there was a lump on top and a hole below. Pressed further about sexual shape and "motive," Moore responded: "When you slice a walnut, that's the form you find." Still, our strategies of process, labor and repetition among them, work for what Russell Edson describes as the ideal prose poem: "a small, complete work, utterly logical within its own madness." He's come to understand his process as "dreaming awake." If we overlook the easy misunderstandings/manipulations of his ideas, what can we say about the prose poem's long interest in the unconscious as a creative vehicle?

PJ: I guess you could argue that if you privilege the unconscious, it makes sense you'll be attracted to prose. Remember that the word *verse* comes from the Latin *verto,* to turn, so if you're a verse poet, even if you rely on the unconscious, as of course you must, your line breaks or metrical choices, the various twists or turns you adopt, will eventually come into play. I like to think that Rimbaud didn't consciously choose the prose poem, but that, in his attempt to make himself a vehicle for the unconscious, prose naturally presented itself. Ironically, he had to go deep into his own unconscious to escape from himself. "For *I* is an other," he said. "If brass wakes a trumpet, it is not its fault." I'm sure the Surrealists were aware of this possibility of prose. Perhaps the freedom poets feel with the prose poem comes from this opportunity to surrender to the chance operations of the unconscious, instead of having to write with all the great versifiers of Western Civilization looking over their shoulders.

SJ: The prose poem has earned considerable recognition of late: magazine allocation and prizes, among them your *Miracles & Mortifications,* which received the 2001 James Laughlin Award. Do you think, as some have said, that *The Prose Poem: An International Journal* single-handedly began a new prose-poem renaissance?

PJ: If that were true, then I would be a visionary. How nice! But, in fact, there was prose-poem activity in journals way before I came along. Steve Wilson was publishing a journal a few years before mine; Greg Boyd was always receptive to prose poems in his *Asylum Annual;* and in 1985 Karen Donovan and Walker Rumble began *Paragraph Magazine,* and, to me, paragraphs look a hell of a lot like prose poems. Over the last twenty years other journals have done special issues on the prose poem.

But I think my journal did give people permission to write prose poems. I noticed that many poets who were writing both verse and prose poetry turned exclusively to the prose poem when they saw it was being taken more seriously. Also, I was fortunate that Bly, Edson, Simic, Naomi Shihab Nye, David Ignatow, and Sybil James came on immediately as contributing editors, and then Morton Marcus joined up later. These people gave legitimacy to the journal and made it easier to distribute. Now it's common to see prose poems in magazines and books, though I think poets have misunderstood the so-called freedom of prose poetry. Edson once said that the problem with most poems is that there is too much language chasing too little of an idea. Every poet, especially every prose poet, should have that taped over his desk.

SF: You have said that poets have misunderstood the "so-called freedom of prose-poetry." The truly bad children will ignore us, but what do you think they should understand?

PJ: While editing my journal, I was irked by the lack of discipline in the prose of the same poets who would bring much higher standards to their verse poetry. Also, mistakenly, many poets think the prose poem gives them permission to write more and faster with little revision. I can't tell you how many times I heard, "If you don't like these poems, I've got a hundred more." Indeed, they did. Unfortunately, the prose poem offers what appears to be an easy form for poets who don't want to work hard. They think, "Wow, I can just sit back, look out the window, and be clever. And I don't even have to worry about line breaks."

SF: With all the historical and biographical allusions in *Miracles & Mortifications,* it's certainly clear you worked hard on that book, so you must have been "pretty happy" when it received the 2001 James Laughlin Award from the Academy of American Poets. I'm wondering how that award has changed your life?

PJ: I was really honored and surprised when *Miracles & Mortifications* won the Laughlin Award, and I was pleased when a reviewer said that it was a book James Laughlin would have loved. But the award itself hasn't changed my day-to-day life because I tend not to do many readings or to socialize as much as other poets do. I find that between my teaching and my family (and we just had a new baby) I have very little time to do anything, and my undergraduates would be more impressed if I were a contestant on *The Weakest Link* or eating a pig's eye on *Fear Factor*. Moreover, I will always be indebted to the Academy of American Poets for placing 10,000 copies of *Miracles* into the hands of poetry lovers. That's mind-boggling. And I'm also grateful to the judges for choosing a book of prose poems from such a small press. I've judged a few contests, so I realize that that there is very little that separates the final manuscripts. I'm very aware that the poetry gods have blessed me.

Interview with Peter Johnson by David Cass

David Cass: In your essay "The Prose Poem and the Comic," you say that the reason so many comic sensibilities are attracted to the prose poem, as opposed to verse, has to do with the "paradoxical nature of the prose poem, the way it so willingly embraces opposites." Would you say that it is the form of the prose poem itself that is mainly responsible for inspiring this yoking of opposites and the comic situations which develop, or is it the tradition of the prose poem which makes it a fertile ground for such exploration?

Peter Johnson: It's hard to say why the prose poem seems predisposed toward comedy. Perhaps many prose poets are comic poets because they studied the tradition and were influenced by poets like Max Jacob, Zbigniew Herbert, Julio Cortazar, and all those great poets in Michael Benedikt's *The Prose Poem: An International Anthology.* I only have my own experience to go by. Why was I attracted to the prose poem? Why did I decide to write them? I have always been attracted to gray areas of literature. My MA thesis was a translation of and introduction to Prudentius' *Psychomachia,* a 4th-century Latin text. It was written in a pagan form (Vergilian Latin), but embraced Christian content (a battle between the virtues and vices). The heartbeat of that text sounds when those two forces play off each other. Similarly, I wrote my dissertation on black humor in the novels of John Hawkes. Again, opposites converging. When does humor become black? Who can say? Put five people in front of a large window at 4 a.m. and ask them to raise their hands when it's sunrise. Everyone will have a different interpretation. So there's a side of me that's comfortable in the midst of opposites. But I also have always been fascinated by surrealism and Dada and shorter genres, so imagine my glee when

I came across Benedikt's anthology. But my experience isn't some blueprint for being a prose poet. I have certain interests and obsessions, a certain disposition and certain predispositions, that were probably always looking for an outlet. Instead of the sonnet, the prose poem presented itself to me. I felt freed from the tyranny of the line which I had studied ad nauseam for what seemed like my entire life, and I could finally speak in a more natural way (at least to me), instead of writing all the bad verse poetry I was writing.

DC: Benedikt's anthology obviously made a great impression on you. You must have felt as if you were looking into a crystal ball—reading your own future. But I'm wondering whether it was Benedikt's anthology that marked a critical change in your writing, steering you toward the prose poem, or whether it was some other factor. Furthermore, what was your experience like when you first experimented with the prose poem?

PJ: When I first "experimented" with the prose poem I didn't know I was writing prose poems. I was fooling around with character sketches. I had been translating the Greek writer Theophrastus, so I started to write a few comic character sketches, three of which are in *Pretty Happy!* When I sent them to journals, some meathead informed me that I was too influenced by Russell Edson, whom I had never heard of. So believing that I should at least read the people I'm influenced by I sought out Edson's work, and one thing led to another, until I came upon Benedikt's anthology and began to see that the prose poem had a long history of stealing from other genres like the character sketch, the epistle, the penseé, and so on.

But to speak more generally about influences like that, as I said before, we all have predispositions to certain ways of thinking and expressing ourselves, and if we keep our eyes open and are patient, those forms will present themselves to us. That's probably what happened to me and the prose poem. It wasn't something I thought about. In fact, it wasn't very cool to be a prose poet when I began writing them. They were very hard to publish. You felt as if you should sign up for some Prose Poets Anonymous self-help group, each session beginning with someone saying, "I am a prose poet," whereupon the audience, most likely wearing paper bags over their heads, would sympathetically nod.

How did I feel when I first started writing prose poems? I felt freed up, but this sense of freedom was quickly followed by frustration when I realized that freedom in poetry comes at a high price. It was then that I realized I had to create the compression and tension I associate with poetry by trying different ways to make those leaps Bly speaks of in his famous essay "Looking for Dragon Smoke." By now, I hope I have internalized some kind of form that suits my temperament. Edson once joked that now there is The Peter Johnson Prose Poem, and even if some people think The Peter Johnson Prose Poem stinks, I appreciate that comment.

DC: Speaking of "The Peter Johnson Prose Poem," I'd like to turn our attention to your book *Miracles & Mortifications*. You talked earlier about your comfort with oppositions, and I see that comfort working thematically throughout your poems. For example, in the second part of your book, "Travels with Oedipus," the persona comes into contact with historical figures from Western Civilization, both the heroes and the villains, and in each case the comedy undercuts grand narratives associated with these people. Interestingly, the comedy often humanizes the people behind the myths—Socrates has a booger in his nose; Hemingway knocks a trout out with a head-butt; a boy Hitler pretends to be a weathervane and whimsically gazes at the stars. Was that a conscious process, or do you think that comedy, in its essence, reveals the truth of the human condition, that every human being, regardless of their fame or infamy, is ultimately just as uncertain and fallible as the next guy?

PJ: Comedy involves contradiction and juxtaposition, both of which are inherent in life, so the human situation, whether it's now or in the days of the caveman, was there. I just had to pay attention to it. There are myths or grand narratives handed down to us about huge historical and literary characters and events, but we have the right to personalize those grand narratives, which is what I did. In a way, though, those portraits are not fabrications. I'm sure Socrates stunk to high heaven and could have easily been spotted with a booger in his misshapen nose. We also could easily imagine Hemingway, drunk, headbutting a trout. But, of course, I'm making fun of these guys, too. *Miracles* worked for me in two ways. First, I was going through a period where I was battling with my teenage son, so I decided to take us on a tour of history, trying to teach him a few lessons. The models were already there: *Don Quixote, Candide, Bill and Ted's Excellent Adventure,* Poindexter and Mr. Peabody from *The Rocky and Bullwinkle Show.* The clash of the high and low in me creates the comedy, and I was constantly juxtaposing high ideas and language with the streetwise language and perspective of my son. I read a lot of biographies when writing these poems and many of the details were taken from them—the serious details that idealize these characters. The comic parts occur when I pretend I'm there. Have you ever been around famous people or "big thinkers"? They often walk around with their zippers down and can be very big jerks.

And this is where the second impulse to write these poems came from. I have this huge respect for the western canon of literature. I really believe in developing a historical sense. I had a classical education at a Jesuit high school, studied Latin and Greek, even in college, and always believed, or I should say, hoped that we could become better people by studying great figures and their ideas. I very much want to make sense of the world and to use these grand narratives as a guidebook. But there's a whole other side of me that is skeptical of grand narratives and hero worship. No doubt, if I had lived in ancient Greece, one minute I would have been sitting mesmerized at Socrates' feet, while the next making fart noises when he was about to arrive at a startling conclusion. I often think my second impulse is the truer one.

I like to think that many of the figures in *Miracles* would have appreciated the book's humor. I like to believe that the ability to laugh at oneself is a prerequisite for genius. If it isn't, I prefer not to be told so. But I didn't think about this stuff when I was writing the book. Again, my initial desire was to work through a difficult period with my son, to write something we could both laugh at because my son has a great sense of humor. It was a place to start, so that we wouldn't tear off each other's heads. The bonus for me was that I also got a chance to review my entire education. There are hundreds of allusions in these poems. I originally kept notes that I was going to append to the back, as Eliot did in *The Waste Land*, but I felt too self-conscious doing that; it was killing the spontaneity of the poems.

DC: In Tony Hoagland's essay "How to Talk Mean and Influence People," he writes, "American Poetry still believes, as romantics have for a few hundred years, that a poem is a straightforward autobiographical testimony to, among other things, the decency of the speaker." Do you think the prose poem, because of its subversive nature, suffers less from this belief than verse?

PJ: It's important to note that Hoagland stipulates what he means by meanness. If I understand him right, to be "mean" isn't to demolish people or social conventions just for the fun of it. I don't think he sees the writer as being superior. The speaker can be decent, but if you're too decent, as Hoagland points out, you may not be able "to set free the ruthless observer in all of us, the spiteful angel who sees and tells, unimpeded by nicety or second thoughts."

I agree with him that our current literary culture of pleasantness makes it impossible to deal with many of its complexities and paradoxes. But you can go too far the other way, too. In the course I'm currently teaching on black humor and contemporary poetry, we've come across poets who sometimes fail because they're just mean. Bukowski can be a great offender here; Catullus, too, who I think influenced a lot of contemporary comic poets. I love Catullus's invectives, but often all you're left with is rage. In contrast, a poet like Ginsberg in "America," a very funny poem by the way, saves himself when, after attacking America, he says, "It occurs to me that I am America." Hoagland's narrator in *What Narcissism Means to Me* similarly often accepts responsibility for the mess he describes around him. He makes fun of duplicitous people and cliché-ridden New and Old Age mini-grand narratives, but he also makes us laugh at the narrative voice in many of those poems. In short, if the satiric or "mean" poet doesn't bring a certain humility to the table, then he's in trouble.

How does all this relate to the prose poem? That's a tough one, since I think the prose poem has been appropriated by the kind of literary culture I often criticize. Twelve years ago, I couldn't give my journal away. Now it's hard to pick up a book of poems and not see a prose poem. In a sense, at least in this country, the prose poem was always thought to be a marginal genre, so it was the perfect form for someone who wanted to write like Catullus or Nicanor Parra. It was fun to be excluded from the Poetry Party. It got the edge up in you, fostered a little anger, which can be a very positive emotion in poetry. Anger can crack open the door to the authentic, and, really, that's enough for most of us.

DC: Your new book, *Eduardo and "I"*, a darkly comic book, in some ways is a continuation of the critique that took place in *Miracles*. Yet unlike in *Miracles*, where the target was oftentimes grand narratives of Western Civilization, in *Eduardo* your sight is aimed on contemporary American culture. And you also seem to target yourself more, your own contradictions, using a humor that is much darker and existential.

PJ: That question assumes that Eduardo, the main character of the first section, is a sort of alter ego—the worst side of me, the anxious, obsessive side. But Eduardo is also much more than that. This book was written at a very odd time for me. On September 2, 2001, I learned that *Miracles* had received the James Laughlin Award, then nine days later the Twin Towers fell, then ten months later we had another child. The book was begun shortly before 9/11 and finished in the summer of 2003, during which time I was emotionally all over the place. The character of Eduardo, who makes up the first section of the book, gave me the opportunity to grapple with certain issues. The first poem of Eduardo's section has a sentence that reads, "For once, the eye before the 'I,'" by which I meant, that the overriding narcissism of American culture momentarily vanished when we were visually confronted by explosions and Americans leaping from fiery skyscrapers. Unfortunately, Eduardo is still self-obsessed, making him distasteful even as he is entertaining. I guess I'm saying that Eduardo is a cultural artifact as well as a literary persona. As an aside, he also exemplifies another obsession of mine: the double in literature, from Poe's William Wilson, to Borges' "I," to Berryman's Henry, and so on.

In the second section of the book, an "I" appears who is somewhat autobiographical but still a persona. This section, written after the baby was born, also begins with an allusion to 9/11. The rest of the book chronicles how the narrator tries to make sense of an increasingly absurd world, very often finding consolation in his wife and children. All of this, of course, sounds very planned and "literary," but in fact the first version of the book was very disorganized and emotionally diffuse. I didn't have a clue what I was doing. But after I finished it, I set it aside for a time, then returned to it, and began to see a pattern. Fortunately, I think I was able to keep the raw emotion of the first draft in the revision. There are twenty-four poems is each section, and I think the book, in general, follows a structural and emotional logic.

DC: Again you mention the importance of putting the "eye" before the "I," especially in regards to reacting to such a horrific event as 9/11; in fact, you say that it is the only way for one to react "authentically." I'm wondering how you, as the writer, make sense of your personas' reactions to the absurd world that they inhabit. On the one hand, your personas exhibit a remarkable alienation. On the other hand, there seems to be a real sense of community, a shared absurd world that seems to provide for everyone. Take, for example, your prose poem "Neighbors." At one point the narrator threatens to kill the "local loony" for screaming at his infant. In the next instant they've become "good friends," and the narrator follows the man everywhere, even though he "can't make sense of his mumblings." Do you think that, in a strange way, alienation has the power to unite?

PJ: Well, we are all in the same situation; we just respond to it differently. Eduardo is alienated but because of his inability to see contingencies and his insufferably overdeveloped id, we find it impossible to sympathize with him. In contrast, the guy you refer to in "Neighbors," is harmless, and for all we know might be closer to the truth than we are. The poet and the loony have always shared the same bed, and it's often hard to discern who's who. They are both outsiders. Whether or not "alienation has the power to unite" is another question, though we'll certainly find out after this last election.

DC: I see what you mean about the poet having to be a bit of an outsider, but these days it seems as if poets aren't just outsiders, they're completely ignored. William Carlos Williams wrote: "It is difficult / to get the news from poetry / yet men die miserably every day / for lack / of what is found there." In this Orwellian day and age when the average person is constantly bombarded with advertisements and 24-hour cable and news that is increasingly from a very limited number of sources, how can the poet maintain his distance and still compete for the attention of potential readers?

PJ: For one thing, there will never be that many readers of poetry, so to lose sleep over that situation is pointless. I agree with you, though, that it is very difficult to promote your work and maintain a distance from the nonsense, but you have to try. For me, it is impossible to write anything worthwhile or to maintain an edge if I'm constantly worrying about this grant or that award or who needs to like me or how many readings I'm going to attend. If you want to be a plumber, you have to accept that you'll eventually end up with arthritis in your back and knees. As a poet, once you start humiliating yourself for short-term praise, you might as well hang it up.

And yet who doesn't want to be famous? Even I'd like to be on the cover of *Rolling Stone*. Just picture me with my shirt off in a leather vest and black beret, sporting tattooed, creatine-enhanced pectorals and biceps, a headline reading, "The New High Priest of Poetry"—an image which is as silly, not to mention as visually upsetting, as the fantasy behind it. In short, I don't really feel sorry for the plight of the poet. Many of us are professors and paid well for what we do. Many of us have become too soft to be very emotional, and if you don't feel strongly about anything, all that's left is to write about language. But, in spite of all of the above, writing and reading poetry is worth it for those moments when you come across a poem or, if you're lucky, a book that forever changes you. We all hope to read, or, even better, to write such a poem. It can happen.

Interview with Peter Johnson by Jamey Dunham

Jamey Dunham: The very title of your recent collection *Rants and Raves: Selected and New Prose Poems* continues a tradition of seemingly contradictory declarations in your work from the subtly paradoxical *Pretty Happy!* to the overt *Miracles & Mortifications.* Readers of your poetry have no doubt come to understand such contradictions often turn out to be false, that the true significance of such dichotomies lies in exploring the oft overlooked common ground. Even the subtitle, *Selected and New Prose Poems,* hints at some culminating moment, while at the same time conceding the poetry itself is moving on; the passenger waking to take in their destination even as the train is pulling out of the station.

Still, the publication of *Rants and Raves* offers an important opportunity to reflect on the considerable accomplishments and contributions you have made within the form. I have even read that Russell Edson has coined the term, "The Peter Johnson Prose Poem." I wonder how you view your work at this stage in your career and if you are able to recognize your own take on the form?

Peter Johnson: It was intimidating to do a "Selected and New." On one hand, I wondered if I had added something significant to the genre; on the other hand I was afraid to discover I hadn't. Finishing a "Selected" and realizing your life's work has basically stunk, or having a critic point it out, is like being married to a woman for forty years, who on your deathbed says that you were not only a jerk but lousy in bed.

JD: Are you pleased with the book?

PJ: I am. I especially like the "New" section. Most "New" sections of

"Selected" volumes are anemic. I had accumulated about forty poems for a new book, which were "complaints"—mild and not-so-mild invectives. But after rereading them I felt the conceit was becoming a bit tiresome and working against itself, and if the conceit wore me down, I knew readers would feel the same. So I chose the best twenty-four. In a sense, *Rants and Raves* includes a chapbook of sorts.

JD: For me, the most satisfying part of reading any "Selected" is the opportunity to consider the poems in relation to one another; trace the ancestral lines and mark new branches or areas of growth. As I read through the selections in *Rants and Raves* I was continually surprised at the ways in which poems I had previously read changed dramatically when considered in relation to one another. I felt the book I was reading was something new and that I was seeing each poem and section with fresh eyes. Could you talk a bit about how you went about choosing and arranging the poems for *Rants and Raves*?

PJ: I've come to trust in my intuition and I am a fan of improvisation, so I just kept rereading the poems from previous books, trying to let the "Selected" develop its own rhythm, so that one poem from each book would lead naturally into the next, and so the last poem of each book would foreshadow the first poem of the next one. Happily, I had the perfect bookends. *Rants and Raves* begins with "Pretty Happy!" and ends with a new poem called "Happy." In short, I think *Rants and Raves* has an interesting symmetry to it, which came about from the poems speaking to each other rather than having an artificial structure imposed on them.

JD: And what of the title? As I mentioned you seem to have an obsession for the gray areas between opposite concepts like miracles and mortifications and opposing characters like Eduardo and "I," and another reviewer has remarked how the "pretty" in "Pretty Happy!" tends to undermine or at least qualify the happiness. You also have a fascination for the ampersand in *Miracles & Mortifications* and *Eduardo & "I."* I was surprised to see it missing in *Rants and Raves*.

PJ: Yes, I've spoken about my fascination for gray areas. In one sense, I've always wished I could be someone who was so far right or left that I'd never doubt myself. That must be comforting. But nothing interesting or authentic happens outside of the gray areas. In fact, a lot of bad things occur. There's no room for absolutes in poetry, and poetry that is driven by inflexible theories is doomed. I just finished reading an essay by the recently deceased philosopher Leczak Kolakowski, called "In Praise of Inconsistency," where he points out how the consistent mind, though very efficient, is responsible for a lot of historical horror shows. The trick is to be comfortable with uncertainty. To embrace it, if possible.

JD: And why the title *Rants and Raves,* and why did you suddenly discard your signature ampersand?

PJ: The title is very personal. It sums up my daily inner struggles, suggesting the ongoing dialectic between cynicism (rants) and idealism (raves). Rereading my work I realized that most of my poems reflect this dialectic, and much of the humor in my prose poems comes from an everyman torn between cynicism and idealism. I really wanted to keep the ampersand but my friend, Richard Elkington, who designs my books, developed a neat cover that utilized old worn-out Underwood typewriter keys, and it didn't work well visually with the ampersand.

JD: If you don't mind, I'd like to return to my first question about how you view your legacy and if you think there is something called "The Peter Johnson Prose Poem."

PJ: Great questions but hard to answer without sounding like a narcissist. I'd like to think that one day I will be attending a special "Peter Johnson" literary conference in Key West, and a young man in a seersucker suit will describe how my work moved the prose poem in a new direction, and how I single-handedly changed American poetry, whereupon I will be carried outside on the shoulders of participants and treated to a night of drunken revelry. But chances are, I'll have to sneak into a similar Key West conference on another poet and upon leaving be struck by a pig's head hurled from a passing pickup. In short, who knows how I'll be received. To be honest, at this point in my life, I don't care. I could stop writing prose poems tomorrow and feel pretty happy about what I've done.

And is there a Peter Johnson prose poem? Yes, I think so. There has to be. Just as there has to be or will be a Jamey Dunham prose poem. If you keep writing and paying attention to what you're doing and are hard on yourself, you can't help but move away from influences and develop your own style. Whether that style has something to offer is another question. But I think we all know when we've done something good. It's a nice feeling when you don't need outside validation.

JD: Let's talk about your readership for a moment. The prose poem has enjoyed a tremendous surge in popularity, thanks in no small part to the success of your poetry and *The Prose Poem: An International Journal*. And yet, as Jacob stated in his preface to *The Dice Cup*, "I hardly know of any poet who's understood what it's all about...." If *Rants and Raves* truly does represent a significant moment for the American prose poem, and I think it does, how do you reconcile that awareness with a complimentary yet unengaged readership?

PJ: You can't. I don't think anyone has too big of a readership, and younger poets are more attracted to personalities than to books. This became very clear to me at the AWP in New York. I was supposed to be on a prose-poem panel organized by Julia Johnson, but something happened and I couldn't make it to New York until the next day. I heard the panel was a success and had a respectable attendance. But the day I arrived I stopped by a prose-poem panel that had Kim Addonizio, Bob Hicok (who I think was a no-show) and some other poets. There had to be 200–300 people in the room. I looked around and didn't notice a soul. Don't get me wrong, I like Addonizio's books and especially Hicok's early work, but I was baffled by why they were on a prose-poem panel, and why there were so many people there. I honestly think people came to see Addonizio, who has somehow become a celebrity. Young poets have grown up in this celebrity-crazed world, and it has seeped into the poetry scene.

So what do you do with all this information? Get mad? Make long speeches about the death of poetry? Personally, I'm more amused than anything by the current poetry scene. It is what is. Who cares? You just try to do the best work you can and maintain some integrity.

People will notice at some point if your poems are good. Even the most narcissistic and sycophantic poet wants to read good poems. I mean, bad poems are painful to read.

JD: In addition to your collections of poetry you've published a collection of short stories, *I'm a Man,* and two young adult novels, *What Happened* and *Loserville. What Happened* was awarded The Paterson Prize, among other recognitions, and yet I'm guessing the young adult genre suffers from some of the same issues of readership as prose poetry. Have you found this to be the case?

PJ: The great thing about young adult literature is that it actually has a huge readership, and I've loved going into high schools where 300 kids have read and discussed my book. They ask the most unexpected questions and sometimes point out things I never saw. One teacher who used my first novel in three of his classes for "at-risk boys" sent me their comments, and one kid wrote, "Finally a book that doesn't suck." It doesn't get any better than that.

JD: Does writing fiction deepen or somehow strengthen your understanding of prose poetry? What do you personally make of the apparent obsession to trace a line where one genre ends and the other begins?

PJ: It's the opposite for me. I think writing prose poetry is the best apprenticeship for a fiction writer. My first novel, not surprisingly, was described as a long prose poem, or series of prose poems. Most fiction, like most prose poetry, is severely overwritten. Being a prose poet made me tighten up my fiction. My novels are very short and intense. I like that, though the market rewards the big fat novels. Read *Twilight*. I could have cut that novel in half, especially the dialogue. If you ever want to get information out of someone, strap him into a chair and read long passages of dialogue from *Twilight*.

JD: Like YA literature, the audience for the prose poem and the number of people writing them has seen a dramatic rise. Are you at all skeptical about the current flood of prose poems washing up in journals across the country that only few short years ago would never have opened their pages to the form?

PJ: The good news is that many journals publish prose poems now. Younger poets have no idea how hard it was to have editors read your prose poetry twenty years ago unless you were already an established verse poet. But I do think poets will never really get it that you have to be hard on yourself if you write prose poems.

JD: While we're on the subject of the literary scene, let's discuss the intricacies of the business side of things for a moment. When *Miracles & Mortifications* won The Laughlin Award you were immediately thrust to the forefront of the contemporary poetry scene. It must have been gratifying to see your work recognized at such a level, but I can also imagine you felt a substantial pressure to follow up that success with an equally strong and successful book. The resulting collection *Eduardo & "I"* was in many respects more ambitious than its predecessor and yet it was not met with the same fanfare. You have stated in previous interviews your distaste for self-promotion and your reluctance towards the rigors of the reading circuit. What have you learned about literary success as it pertains to the merit of the work as opposed to say the business of being a professional poet?

PJ: I was stunned by the Laughlin Award. I didn't know any of the judges, and I always assumed those awards were inside jobs. It was gratifying to know that an unknown guy could still have a chance, and the people at the Academy of American Poets were very gracious to me and my wife when I went to New York to read. I'm sure the Academy took some heat when a book of prose poems by a relatively obscure poet won.

But I'd been around long enough to realize that all the finalists could have won. A lot is luck. I understand that my book went unnoticed, and then one person became a strong advocate for it. Afterwards I can't tell you how many people said I was now poised to move to a "new level." They all kept using that phrase, and I didn't know what the hell they were talking about. I knew the award wasn't going to change my life because we'd just had a child, so between him and my teaching the only level I was rising to was the second floor of my house to change his diapers. Ironically, I think *Eduardo & "I"* did go to another level and that it was much better than *Miracles*. It had hundreds of allusions and was exhausting to write. After I finished it I felt like going on a Valium drip for a month. But you can't expect to win the Laughlin Award every time you write a book.

JD: So what was the "new level" everyone was talking about?

PJ: Again, it was the celebrity level. I guess I was supposed to start a blog and travel coast-to-coast, reading my poems to five people at various Borders bookstores. Or now that my name was out there I should have started a few fights at conferences or cheated on my wife with a number of distressed younger women—anything to keep people talking about me. I don't mean to be a jerk but I honestly don't know how people do all this socializing unless they don't have kids, significant others, or even pets.

JD: You have previously mentioned the frustration you feel when you read earlier poems that could benefit from revision. Let's look at the first section of the book, the poems taken from your first collection *Pretty Happy!* How did those poems hold up for you?

PJ: I'm very fond of that book but I can see many influences in it. Sometimes I think the book is like a history of the prose poem from Theophrastus's character sketches (which I had translated) to Simic's little gems in *The World Doesn't*, though I still see my own preoccupations with father-son relationships, the nonsense of the poetry world ("The Genius," "Poet Laureate," and "19th-Hole Condom Poem"), and also my interest in questions of theodicy. The crucial poem in that volume was the last one, "The Millennium." It changed everything for me and was the only poem I wrote in longhand. I was in Buffalo visiting family, and on Christmas Eve I went sledding with my oldest son, who was then about ten. We went flying over a snowboarding hump and when I landed I heard a crack and knew I had broken my back. I spent two days in the hospital, and then a few more at my mother's, heavily medicated. I took in all the images around me—the Christmas tree, my niece's various Barbie Dolls and other presents, and began to jot them down, trusting in my imagination to juxtapose and make sense of them. That was the first time I relied mostly on intuition. It was an exhilarating experience and provided me with a method of composition, or at least a place to start when writing future prose poems.

JD: *Pretty Happy!* opens with two of my favorite prose poems from your early work: the title poem "Pretty Happy!" and "Nettles." The two poems arranged together offer a perfect lens through which to view the work that follows. We see the self-deprecating wise guy alongside the romantic artist who can't help but cast himself and his surroundings in a classical light. Do you feel your current poems are still born to some degree from this duality?

PJ: Yes, always the constant friction between the idealist and the cynic. I'm constantly disappointed in myself and others yet also believe things can get better. Anyone can be a wise guy, but whiners are boring, and so are their poems because they have no resonance.

JD: The second section of *Rants and Raves* consists of poems from *Miracles & Mortifications.* The symmetry of the two sections, "Travels with Gigi" and "Travels with Oedipus," is as apparent in these selections as in the original collection; however, this time I was more aware of how the odysseys speak not just to your relationships with your wife and son but also to your relationship with poetry. You've mentioned in previous interviews the contradictory nature of the poems in this collection, the grand historical allusions offset by self-deprecating humor and vulnerability. The poems in this section are tighter, more ambitious and ultimately more confident than the poems they proceed and yet they go to great lengths to humanize the speaker, often tripping him to prevent him from reaching any pedestals. Were you aware of this at the time these poems were written?

PJ: Some of the decisions were conscious. I love unreliable narrators, so I wanted them in both sections. But I wanted the reader to like the narrators, to understand that they were doing the best they could. One narrator is dealing with a nymphet, and the other, an incorrigible teenager. As I've said, I had my literary precedents. For the love poems there were many, especially *Lolita,* Ovid, Catullus, and Andreas Capellanus. For the son poems, *Don Quixote, Bill and Ted's Excellent*

Adventure, and *The Rocky and Bullwinkle Show.* Most of the poems in *Miracles* are mock heroic. I love that genre. But the personal was also there. The love poems were inspired by my wife's eroticism, or at least how I perceive that eroticism, though, unlike Gigi, my wife is the least neurotic person I know. The son poems were inspired by my son's difficult teenage years. But you're right to say that both of those sections are really about language, and Nabokov and Max Jacob showed me the way. I invented words, joined the strangest phrases and images, and had fun playing with double entendre. In this sense, the book is a tribute to how elusive yet suggestive language can be, and how a writer can manipulate an audience with it.

JD: There is a palpable shift in tone and style between the selections from *Miracles & Mortifications* and *Eduardo & "I"*. While structurally there are some similarities in these poems to the previous sections, there is also an underlying darkness, a starker contrast between the heavy and the light. What was the motivation or driving force behind the poems in this collection? Was it personal or artistic? Can the two ever be entirely separated?

PJ: I think *Eduardo & "I"* is my best book. There is still humor, but you're right to say it's very dark. The "Eduardo" section was my response to 9/11. To me the character of Eduardo is a cultural artifact, the embodiment of narcissism in our country. While the whole world is falling apart, he's more interested in getting tattoos. He's really my dark side. It's a very disturbing section, and yet you have to laugh at Eduardo as you would at all those whack-jobs sharing embarrassing details of their lives on reality TV shows. When I wrote that book I was kind of giving up on people and institutions, but, at the same time, as I said, a year after 9/11 we had another child, a little boy. That's where the second section comes in, and the "I" is more autobiographical. That "I" is still struggling, especially with questions of theodicy, but you can see how family saves him, how playing with his little kid, or imagining his teenage son telling the "whole damn neighborhood just how much he loves [him]," makes it possible for him to get up in the morning. And let's not forget the importance of sex, "those endless nights in damp and twisted sheets." If I had written only *Eduardo & "I"* and then got hit by a bus, I could have died happy.

JD: So who is the Peter Johnson who wrote the poems found in the "New" section and do you feel these poems would be possible without the poems that preceded them?

PJ: The Peter Johnson of the "New" section was angry at the Bush administration, angry at the general idiocy of Americans, and angry at the world of Po-Biz. I consider most of the new poems to be invectives. Some were painful to write, others quite a bit of fun. The invective is an underappreciated genre, and you don't see it too much anymore. It's important to note that the epigraph for *Rants and Raves* is the title of the Ramones' last album, *Adios Amigos*. That's the way I felt. I thought it was time to say goodbye and go quietly away. But then I couldn't help but close the book with "Y'all come back now," knowing I might change my mind. No matter how much you feel as if you're pissing into the wind when you kill yourself writing poems not many people will read, something brings you back. Maybe you go to a reading and hear a terrific poem. Maybe a student tells you, almost in tears, about when he first fell in love with poetry. In my Introduction to Literature course, for the last week of classes I have my freshmen read Dana Gioia's essay, "Can Poetry Matter?" Then I ask them to choose their favorite short poem and recite it to the class and write a one-page paper, explaining why the poem matters. Their responses are often very moving. I guess what I'm saying is that when you can ignore all the nonsense associated with contemporary American poetry, you eventually see that poetry does matter, that it can really change people's lives.

JD: As you look ahead now, do you like where you see yourself and your poetry going?

PJ: I'm not sure where I'm going. As we discussed earlier, I've been writing literary young adult novels, which are considered "crossover novels," that is novels for adults too. I would like to find some way to merge the prose poem and the young adult novel. I'd like to write a novel in prose poems, but make it as literary as any of my other books. I've also begun to edit my correspondence with Edson from 1992 to 2007. I think I have about 350 letters from him. We'll see. Right now, I need a short break. In 2011, I will have published seven books in eleven years with a heavy teaching load and a little boy who was born when I was fifty. I need to slow things down, and there are a lot of books I've been wanting to read, and new class preparations I'd like to work on. I've always received more pleasure from giving a good class than getting a poem published. I'd also like to get back to taking naps. Edson tells me he's a great napper.

Little Mr. Prose Poem:
Selected Letters from Russell Edson

Little Mr. Prose Poem

In 1992 Russell Edson was as surprised as I was by the enthusiastic response to the inaugural issue of *The Prose Poem: An International Journal,* which I edited for nine years. In fact, I had titled it Volume 1 as a private joke. I had no intention of editing a Volume 2. But what followed was an avalanche of letters from poets who had been toiling for years in the genre, with trashcans full of nasty rejection letters. These poets were not only running out of journals to submit to, but they were also sick of defending the prose poem to editors who knew little about it.

Shortly after the publication of Volume 1, Russell and I began a correspondence that lasted until he died in 2014, though the bulk of the 350 letters I received from him were between 1992 and 2008. There is a gap between the last and penultimate letters that follow, but I wanted to include the last one because it referred to the demise of my journal, which signaled an end to a heady period for the prose poem. I was, quite frankly, burned out. Although Russell sympathized with me, he wanted me to persevere. To him, the journal authenticated what he had spent his life writing. As he said, it made him feel less "isolated," suggesting it was "responsible for making the prose poem almost legitimate." He was also surprised (and pleased) to discover that he had influenced so many poets.

The letters I've annotated here occurred during the early days of the prose poem renaissance when Russell was reentering the poetry world with *The Tunnel: Selected Poems,* and I was trying to get my first book published. He used to say that he spent most of his time in bed, staring at the ceiling, so it was hard to get him out of that supine position to organize a new manuscript. That manuscript eventually ended up being *The Tormented Mirror,* and he speaks often about the frustrating process of finishing and publishing that book.

I've tried to choose letters that highlight his ideas on the writing process and creative impulse. All of what he says is usually brilliant and could be said of poetry in general. You may ask, "Peter, where is your side of the correspondence?" Well, I didn't begin to keep my letters until we had about 100 exchanges. Why? First of all, I didn't think of our correspondence as being public knowledge or part of literary history. Secondly, I had a very different life than Russell. I didn't lie in bed and stare at the ceiling. I taught three different classes per semester, I edited a journal, I was writing and publishing my own work, and I was raising children and coaching their sports. I didn't have time to think about "literary history," until my friend Forrest Gander pulled me aside and said, "Peter, what are doing? Even if you don't think what you have to say is important, your side of the correspondence provides context for Edson's letters." Of course he was right, and after all these years, even I can see that, in some small way, my journal helped to champion the prose poem by providing a home for prose poets who had previously felt ignored.

In a sense, Russell and I were very different people. He called himself "Little Mr. Prose Poem," and he called me "Big Mr. Prose Poem." He was a recluse. Yes, he enjoyed giving readings, yet he approached the travel and necessary pleasantries of these readings with fear and loathing, that is, unless he was reading with friends like James Tate or Charles Simic. In contrast, I seemed to be outgoing, a "people person." But this was an illusion. I started my journal for two reasons: first, to make the prose poem legitimate; second, to contribute to contemporary American poetry without having to leave the house.

I miss Russell. I miss his intelligence and wacky wit. He made me think and laugh, often at the same time. Many of his letters read like long prose poems. He thought like a Russell Edson prose poem, probably just as his father, the cartoonist Gus Edson, conceptualized life in the form of cartoon frames. He was an original, and without him the prose poem probably never would have taken hold in America.

October 14, 1994

Dear Peter,

Just a note. No need to answer.

A literary influence is really a kind of permission that allows us to open something in ourselves.[1] It's there but we're not in touch with it yet. Then one sees a painting, or reads something, or even hears a work of music, and suddenly possibilities begin to be suggested.

Poetry doesn't have to be la-de-da. Nor does it have to be practiced as an oh-so-serious-business, with a self-consciousness that destroys any possibility of the other voice that I seek.

Then there have been those who for some reason have wanted to control the "poetry business." Meddler types like Pound and his aesthetic descendants. Instead of just being satisfied to get their own work written, they become the high priests of what they define as poetry. As far as I'm concerned, poetry is no more sacred than fiction. They are two sides of the same coin.

Besides two novellas and a book of small plays, I've never written anything but prose paragraphs. This, before I ever heard of that strange term, prose poem. This is how I became "Little Mr. Prose Poem."

As of this writing, my book[2] has yet to appear. You changed the date from June to August for the ad in the *Journal*.[3] And now it's mid-October and still no book.

You keep striking so close.[4] Sooner or later something has to happen. One's first book is kind of a giddy experience, to be sure. But disillusionment comes early. After my first I could still barely get into a magazine. Ten years would pass, and then suddenly I had two

---

1. Some of Russell's observations in the letters repeat what he said in my interview with him, but I felt those observations gained more meaning when viewed in the context of a complete letter.
2. *The Tunnel: Selected Poems of Russell Edson,* from Oberlin College Press, 1994.
3. *The Prose Poem: An International Journal.*
4. I was trying to get my first book published, which was eventually called *Pretty Happy!* and was published by White Pine Press in 1997.

publishers in the same year. If one does what one does long enough something will happen. How can it not? This is why I think, far more than talent, the passionate will to write is the important thing. Talent really runs in the streets. We're all talented, but few of us think it important enough to pursue. As for me, I'll just sit on my new ms.[5] I haven't the heart for contests, nor heart for sending stuff out uninvited.

I continue to be amazed at the success of the *Journal*. I really thought your enthusiasm would collapse after the first issue. That perhaps the prose poem was too narrow a genre to keep a magazine going. But the *Journal* has more unity and purpose than most literary magazines. You've proven that the prose poem deserves its own magazine.

Since starting this note Stuart[6] sent me some finished covers of my book. Looks pretty good. Perhaps too good.

Best,

Russell

---

5. *The Tormented Mirror*, eventually published by the U. of Pittsburgh Press in 2001.
6. Stuart Friebert, editor of Oberlin College Press.

November 10, 1994

Dear Peter,

Sorry I missed your call. But Frances[1] related what you said. And I thank you for your good words. I had rather given up on the book.[2] And then it suddenly appeared.

It is true, we work in a very narrow area. And as you say, who the hell reads what we write, anyway? It's very easy to be discouraged. One sort of goes along as in a dream, and then suddenly looking up from one's work one is startled to see how much time has elapsed.

I don't know how to improve a prose poem in the physical way a "line" poem can be made better. This is why I write fast in a hit or miss fashion, without plan or direction. A good much of the pleasure of writing is being surprised. If something comes out whole and realized it's an unplanned surprise. The thing is not to expect too much. To treat each piece as a sketch toward something one will never accomplish. The main idea is to have the freedom to fail, as well as sometimes finding something, though unfinished, wonderful that formed outside of the self-conscious idea of literature.

I can't see any way to improve a book, only the making of editorial picks from stacks of work, most of which will never be offered for publication. The strategy is quantity over quality.

No you are not just a mid-wife. You're the editor of a hot magazine, and you have a ms. ready for publication. You're where the action is. Western culture is run aground, ergo, the prose poem. I know it's frustrating. But the main thing is to have the work. The rest follows. I can sit on my ms. forever, but you need a first book. Incidentally, I haven't published a book since 1985. Oh, forgot, I did publish a small, uneventful novel in 1992. But after my first book, ten years would elapse. Then two books in the same year from Wesleyan and Harper & Row. And so it goes. But that was years

---

1. Russell's wife.
2. *The Tunnel.*

ago before the prose poem had much legitimacy. It's still marginal writing, and perhaps that's why it has so much energy.

I hope to send a good batch of work for you to consider vis-à-vis the next *Journal.*

Best,

Russell

January 6, 1995

Dear Peter,

Night, and cold as a witch's you know what. You wrote back in mid-November. Meanwhile, Christmas and New Year. And so it goes, until it doesn't.

You were talking in your letter about the dangers of narcissism, as you put it, "self-discovery mumbo-jumbo." And that you saw in "An Historical Breakfast"[1] an answer to this malady. Yes, satire, but not purposeful satire. I write to amuse myself, not to change others. Socially angry poems, anti-war poems; poems that are meant to do things violate the creative spirit. The only thing required of the poem is to be. I'm just suggesting that poets ought to have the decency to stay out of their poems. The best poem has an impersonal quality which allows the reader room to dream into the poem.

I hadn't realized, save for mentioning it in your letter, that I haven't published a new book in nine years. So I won't ask you if you've had any luck placing your book. It's too tantalizing. The worst part of publishing a book is getting releases from all the magazines where the work first appeared. Legally it's not necessary, but publishers demand it as part of the process of securing the author's copyright. It's a mess. Sometimes things get so fussy one might almost consider suicide. On the other hand, one decides to go on living just out of petty curiosity. One has choices. One is not entirely helpless. I suppose there is an instinct in all of us to live long enough to take our last breath. Breathing is, after all, like smoking, addictive. Yes, I admit to being addicted to the atmosphere. So, due to the above-mentioned bothers I am in no special hurry to get into the process of another book. Not to mention my pieces are scattered over many a computer disk. Harvesting a book from the various disks is a work in itself. Then there's the task of proofing what comes from the typesetter. All, all too much for one man. Incidentally, on page 109 of *TT* there's a typo, "or"

---

1. Edson prose poem from *The Tunnel*.

instead of "nor," as it was in the original text. I thought of ending it all when I discovered this. But decided a few typos might make a book more authentic. One must lie to oneself to keep going. But the lies must be clever so one does not catch oneself. An undiscovered lie is then a truth. Who knows the difference? Thus truth is anything we believe. And I believe this. It is all rather circular, a merry-go-round of sanity and its otherwise. But we mustn't be too fancy, we know where that leads. Cling to the wooden horse and enjoy the ride.

In the course of this writing I received from Ireland, no less, *Poetry Ireland Review,* "Special North American" issue. It includes a good much of better known poets of the U.S. and Canada, but in the whole thick magazine the only prose poems are mine. Perhaps the prose poem is not as popular as we thought. And perhaps the best reason to be writing them; the best reason for the *Journal.*

I will have materials to show you.

Best for 1995,

Russell

January 30, 1995

Dear Peter,

Reading through the prose poems you sent I can understand your impatience about placing a book. You have the materials. Also reading through my own things of the last weeks, everything in these readings makes good sense. At least for a while. And then suddenly I come awake and see how marginal, how really strange the prose poem is. Don't you sometimes come to this? That we have a strange enthusiasm which may be quite more narrow than we realize. But, what's more interesting than a prose poem in the current world of letters?

Your piece "Like Father, Like Son" is close to the kind of thing I am wont to do. The merging and changing of identities, the reversals. The way it develops into its own conclusion.

The pieces constitute a nice group. I was sort of kidding when I described the miseries of the book publishing process. It is fun to publish a book. But like anything else the thrill gets less and less. Fact is I printed my first little books. And it worked in the sense to leading to "bigger and better things." A reckless use of energy. But it was fun because it didn't have a set purpose. Handsetting type; the letterpress thing seemed as interesting as prose poems at the time. Luck is everything. Luck might be described as coincidence. Being at the right place at the right time. But perhaps it's all been written, and we merely act it out.

As for improving a manuscript, in a sensible world one ought to be able to do that. But having no true objective standards (I wonder if anyone has?) I write around the problem. Write a load of things and pick at the time what seems the better things, and let the others go to hell. And yet, perhaps you've noticed this, certain pieces need time to be properly approached. Which is to say that the work remains strange to its writer. Either the writer matures in understanding, or the piece somehow ripens like a wine or cheese, and one suddenly understands. This is why I say one doesn't want to be too familiar with what one writes. And this is what I like about the prose poem.

I can read your things as if I wrote them. And I can read my own things as if I hadn't written them. The prose poem isn't all tied up in personality. After reading through your things I immediately sat down and wrote a bunch of other things. Endless invention. Perhaps in the future it'll become a tradition that prose poems will not be identified by author. I could even see a book of prose poems containing the work of many writers, but presented as the work of a single author. Or not even that; that it would be understood that the prose poem was so impersonal a form that no writer needed to take credit for it. It would be rather like the harvesting of a plenitude. There may even come a time when people who write prose poems will cease writing them, but meet together and invent them on the spot vocally. But perhaps this is too much to hope for. Meanwhile we work in our private cells writing on disks and paper. But there will come a time when this will be considered rather quaint. People will say, that's how it was done in the old days.

But for now for anybody interested in the prose poem the *Journal* is the center. It's where we all meet. So I'm grateful for all the trouble you've gone to for *TT*. Your enthusiasm has been very encouraging. Apparently, this is true for so many others who continue to support the *Journal* with their work.

Best,

Russell

February 8, 1995

Dear Peter,

It's true, the prose poem wants "normal" speech. And no matter how nutty the poem the language should try to fall as naturally as common talk. The mistake of many beginning prose poem writers is that they don't trust their own imaginations. If they don't trust what they're writing the reader won't. Often they seem to say in so many ways, "I know this is strange stuff but ..." The prose poem wants to deal with strange stuff, but to treat it in the same way and with the same belief as "normal" stuff.

I think what you like about "Pretty Happy"[1] is that nothing seems forced, everything falls naturally, with the baseball bat at the end as the hook. To get to this kind of writing, at least for me, is to write a great deal, and fast. Basically, to lose one's self-consciousness, so that the writing is as natural as any other activity. Getting past oneself.

A lot of my so-called originality is owed to eccentricity and literary isolation. If I've done anything special, anybody could have if they *would* have. It's right there. Everybody has a nutty head. Our job as the rational species is to override this nuttiness. But at a keyboard with nothing to lose, why not enjoy the impersonal parts of our brains? This is what's so good about the prose poem. Having a lower literary ambition than other forms, it allows the writer the freedom to invent. The form doesn't overwhelm and allows content to be everything.

Other magazines run ads, but they get paid for their trouble,[2] speaking of *TT.*

Poetry is a social club. I ain't too social; basically a hermit who writes letters. But I realize now that to move ahead in terms of publishing and other fun things one should become part of the club. Otherwise one waits patiently for the world to find one's work. I guess

---

1. "Pretty Happy" is one of my poems that ended up being the title of my first book.
2. I ran ads for free in *The Prose Poem: An International Journal,* which will be called *TPP* in footnotes that follow this one.

the main thing is to stay "pretty happy," while keeping a baseball bat handy.

Best,

Russell

Truths, Falsehoods, and a Wee Bit of Honesty

March 28, 1995

Dear Peter,

I have been going through *Somebody's Fool*.[1] Am not finished. A lot of mail has piled up here, and I'm trying to put my head together for a big-bucks reading in Indianapolis, which I dread.

To begin with I'm not sure that *Somebody's Fool* is the best title for the collection. It sounds a bit flip. In fact, the actual poem seems somewhat scattered. Perhaps too thought out. I cringe at the idea of someone walking on thumbtacks, even to "keep his mind off his mind," which is an interesting thought.

Thing is, a prose poem needs to be more orderly, more compact than what goes as verse these days. Thus, the prose poem should only include *working* parts. One needs to have the courage to drop "good stuff" for the sake of the whole poem. This is a fault found in many prose poems. The writer refusing to let go of something that's clever and interesting, but doesn't add to the psychological movement of the poem. Anything that doesn't add is a distraction, and robs the poem's reality.[2]

My ideal prose poem is a small, complete work, utterly logical within its own madness. Like for instance your poem "Hell," among others. This poem doesn't seem over-thought. It falls quite naturally. A certain staleness sets in when a prose poem is too slowly written. This is why I like to write fast and much, looking for an organic wholeness. Something that falls with a naturalness no matter how mad the material. Of course you'll say "Hell" was very self-consciously thought out. But it doesn't read like that. Everything in it seems just discovered.

---

1. Original title of my first book before I settled on *Pretty Happy!*.
2. We always went back and forth on this. Although I agreed that the prose poem should be simplicity itself and compact, from editing my journal, I also saw that adhering strictly to that dictum ruled out a lot of very good work. Also, many prose poems by masters of the genre, like Bly, Wright, and Waldrop, are not interested in the kind of wacky logic that characterizes an Edson poem. But note later on how Russell is humble enough to realize all this on his own.

Most people writing prose poems who would be considered at our end of the rainbow know that the prose poem must deal with the strange, that that's its purpose. To deal with dream stuff in conscious language. But often, with this purpose in mind, the author doesn't trust his vision enough, and does too much explaining and scene setting. Simic is a master of simplicity in his line and prose poems. With a few strokes the mood and scene are set. Again, it's a matter of simplicity, of being able to think in a physical way. More gesture than word.

So the prose poem wants to be properly *staged*. To make some kind of whacky physical sense. For instance, in "A Ritual as Old as Time Itself," which is a very good poem, all goes well until the sand gives way under the husband's feet. There's no reason for that to happen, and it loses the reality the rest of the poem has. But the poem needs to break there, and for the husband and wife to change places, which gives the poem its mad design. You may feel I make too much of this, but I only use this as an example of what makes an otherwise original and interesting poem, weak. Why can't the husband simply run out of steam? He's been running up and down the beach for a year. Now it's her turn to fly the marriage kite. Let the reader make of the poem what he or she will. Obviousness is one of my favorite devices. It's not only humorous because it's unexpected, but no one can hide things in the obvious for the reader to find and build on. There should be room for the reader to do something with the prose poem besides simply reading it.

But you see, I'm already re-thinking another man's work. Since the prose poem has no classic model, I can only talk about what I've been doing. And what I've been doing is not necessarily the way. What your MS really needs is to be published.

April 7, 1995. Am just back from Butler U. Talked out. It all went well but I'm tired of talking about writing.³ When I got back I read this big dumb letter that hardly says anything. Oh, well …

Best,

Russell

---

3. Russell always had mixed emotions about readings. He liked the attention and the readings themselves but truly approached the social demands of them with fear and dread.

Peter Johnson

April 15, 1995

Dear Peter,

There ain't no rules for the prose poem. For me, when a poem gets too long (what's the measure?) it gets too prosy. Maybe Yau's[1] poem works. And if it doesn't, so what? The beauty of the prose poem is that it is open to every writer. A real democratic form. I'm so sick of the celebrity poet whose work has less content than their celebrity.

In a certain way I find in my own work I'm fleeing from fiction, and at the same time fleeing from the definition of poetry. And at the same time wanting the narrative power of fiction and the power of dream-thinking as found in poetry. The purpose is of course poetry. But poetry that has no root in fiction is aesthetic mist. And fiction that owes nothing to poetry is not worth the reading. Ergo, for today, the prose poem.

You're right to "be as hard on oneself as possible and avoid sentimentality and self-consciousness...." One way is to write a lot and to abandon most of it. It's an ongoing thing. Magazine or a book publication are merely interruptions in the flow. Writing for me is simply keeping in touch with something I don't know. Yet, there's an aesthetic to it. And again something I don't know.

I was surprised by the people not represented in the Oberlin anthology. I suppose one will always wonder in this way about any anthology. Still, it is odd in light of the poets you mention. And there are large-name poets included who are not known particularly for their prose poems. And yet, a large-name poet like Ignatow who is known for a considerable body of prose poems is ignored. I asked Stuart about this. No answer. Fixel[2] is a sad case. As far as I know he's been undeservedly ignored generally. Others, too.

There are no big bucks in the kind of writing I do. 7% royalty per book doesn't add up to much. One can do a lot better with readings that are offered because of one's books. It's a terrible business.

---

1. Refers to a very long prose poem from my journal written by John Yau.
2. One of the masters of the prose poem, especially the parable.

Has anything happened with Coffee House?[3] This is probably a silly question. Nothing happens. And then suddenly a lot of things happen. Like for instance the death of James Gill[4] (*2PLUS2*). I really don't know why we're born. If we're designed to die, and we are, why not get right to it, and not be born?

Oh, heck …

Russell

---

3. I had sent my manuscript to Coffee House Press.
4. Legendary editor of *2PLUS2*.

September 9, 1995

Dear Peter,

In "Sibling Rivalry," making pretend that I dreamed the piece, I would have been tempted to start it: "I have no older sister, so I'm not surprised when she arrives at my birthday party." I think the word *not* makes it more mysterious and psychologically consistent. Whether I'm right or wrong, it's a very good piece. "The Genius" is also very good. You write the kind of prose poem I've always tried to write. Imagination with logic; let the piece be as nutty as hell, but let it have logic and drama. Even so, the prose poem is a large enough umbrella to fit almost anything under it.

I've asked Jim Tate several times to send work for you to see. He always says he will, but he doesn't. It may be that he doesn't have work to send. I think the last time I mentioned the idea to him was in Rotterdam. I'll try to pin him down when I speak to him again. Charlie S. is also a good friend of his.

One or two magazines won't prove very much about one's work, but the number and quality of the magazines you're appearing in does, in the sense of being publishable, whatever that means. Your work is out there. You might be amazed at the number of frustrated writers who would give anything to have an acknowledgements list you have. I know it's a little like saying to a homely girl, "But you do have beautiful eyes." This magazine publishing is not a little thing. It could be that more people are seeing your work than they might were it locked in a small-press book. Of course a book is the thing to have. And you will. Presently you have good reason to be "Pretty Happy."

It might be postpartum depression, Vol. 4 having just been born.

Incidentally, you asked if a pig's bladder is big, that is, as big as your colleague's head. I don't know about your colleague's head, but everything about a pig is big, including the boar's testicles. Oddly enough I just wrote a piece with an old man suckling a sow's teat for lunch.

Best regards,

Russell

PS: I should really publish a book. But where?

October 9, 1995

Dear Peter,

Got your review and read it with great interest. You are certainly the champion of the prose poem. It was a good idea to begin the piece with that bibliography. Some of the titles are new to me. Obviously in those cases I wasn't asked. But the list does help to show the prose poem is not just a novelty or a lazy man's poetry.

You make the point that the writer looking to publish his first book of prose poems is going to find most doors shut. After all these years the prose poem still remains marginal. But then you ask what if the genre became mainstream. I'm not sure it's the genre that's so much rejected as what the genre can carry, and very often does. I'm amazed that I've been able to publish as much I have. Some of it is pretty grotesque by mainstream standards.

Jonathan Monroe's "a genre that wants out of genre and still finds itself, for all that, inscribed in genre," is rather good.

I like your joking about the only anthology you would truly appreciate would be one that you edited and that carried a lot of your own work. That wouldn't be wrong. And there's the historical precedence of the Benedikt anthology. Just thought, David Young included some of his work in the Oberlin anthology.

It is curious that David Ignatow is absent from the Oberlin anthology, as well as Lawrence Fixel. Incidentally, in the latest *Journal* David has a piece, "The Man Who Fell Apart in the Street As He Walked," which is almost like a poem I wrote, "Oh My God, I'll Never Get Home." Of course he does it better. But you can see we're all writing the one big prose poem. The prose poem is not so much a form as a way of mind.

I reviewed three books of fables in *Parnassus* (Vol. 16, No. 1) under the title, "The Soul of Tales," which gave me a perfect platform to talk about our favorite genre. You may find this of interest vis-à-vis thoughts on the prose poem.

Meanwhile, the "Language Poets" have come out with "The New Prose Poem." So watch your step.

I guess this is the Golden Age, as you put it, of the prose poem. I wonder how it would feel starting to publish now rather than when I did? The world, no matter what one might say, is a lot friendlier to the genre then it was. Speaking of the Golden Age, I like the way you end your review, "No doubt a frightening thought for some hardcore formalists—maybe even for some hardcore prose poets."

Best,

Little Mr. Prose Poem

Peter Johnson

February 26, 1996

Dear Peter,

That's criminal, *The Harvard Review* holding your work that long. There's an unwritten law, eight weeks and that's it. One is free to send one's work elsewhere. Of course you want to be in the magazine, and still hope to. It's just not fair for a magazine to tie up work like that. That's why I will not send cold.

Of the few things I sent to *Verse,* one was finally accepted. Not a very ambitious piece, a piano that shits like an elephant.

Yes, you may use "The Encounter" for the *Journal* ad. You didn't have to ask. And of course I'll be sending new work for you to see.

Sometime back Burning Deck did a chapbook of mine, and the Waldrops[1] send me books every so often. They're good folks and run a fine little press. But I'm not sure they'd go for the expense of a full book. And I wouldn't ask them, anyway. Am beginning to understand that perhaps I don't really want to do another book. Though the materials are here, but the bother attached to publishing a book ... And yet, I almost feel a duty to my previous work to go on with the circus. I've watered the elephants for many a year.

That batch of poems you sent, they lack that hesitation that spoils so many prose poems. When the writer explains too much, not trusting his reader, he's really saying to the reader that the poem is false, that the author doesn't even believe it. When I write belief is not a question. It's a matter of acceptance, that what's appearing on the page is as real as anything else that experience has catalogued.

Every household should have a lawyer[2] under its roof to protect that same household from other lawyers.

My wife broke her ankle last February—a plate, two pins and a small bone graft. The worst part is becoming mobile again. As awful as this

---

1. Rosmarie and Keith Waldrop, poets and editors of Burning Deck Press.
2. My wife is a prosecutor.

was, and she's quite normal now, what happened to you could have been far worse.³ Winter is a dangerous place.

Be well,

Russell

---

3. A cracked rib.

Peter Johnson

March 18, 1996

Dear Peter,

Skipping to the bottom of your letter. I think you've earned the right to be critical. You're a teacher and editor; not to mention also being a writer of the stuff, yourself. You say anyone can write a competent poem, which is probably true. But not everyone is willing to sit alone and do it. Then you use the word "sensibility" as separating the boys from the men. Of course that is the truth of the matter. We probably all have interesting heads, but not all of us can relax the reality of our egos enough to write free of ourselves. It is my pleasure to find something I never thought of on the page.

When I did the NEA poetry panel thing, looking through hundreds of poems, it was as if, most times, I was reading the same poem written by the same writer. The same superficial treatment of experience with little penetration. The triumph of description over creativity.

I wish *Verse* had taken a more ambitious piece. That piano that shits like an elephant (that's its only trick) seems a rather slight piece to represent Little Mr. Prose Poem. But I don't think Mr. Henry[1] tolerates silliness as well as the *Field* folks, who can sometimes seem a little unadventuresome. They asked for work, so I sent four really silly works. They took all four to my surprise. Would it be too far-fetched to consider silliness as an art form? You say *Verse* is giving thirty pages including an intro. by Charlie to the pp section. I hope you don't mind my using pp for prose poem. It simplifies life a little. Life needs that.

You probably still haven't heard from *The Harvard Review*. I'd send the work elsewhere. As for sending work out, I hope to be sending you stuff to see in the next few days. Very new pieces: one about making stew out of a physician; another, a conversation between a woman looking for her unborn baby, and a man trying to count his testicles; a tree that wants to marry a young woman; and an old man

---

1. Brian Henry, the editor of *Verse* at the time, who took that journal to a new level.

looking for a site on his person to grow a new umbilical cord. Four uplifting pieces that need to have their punctuation and reality checks before sending. Of course one must never fall in love with anything one writes. After the fun of the writing one must look upon what one has written as if someone else had written it. Because, in a way, someone else has. This sounds spooky, and it is.

Maybe I can send work with this. If not, soon after.

Glad to hear you're feeling better,

Russell

Peter Johnson

September 20, 1996

Dear Peter

I'm sitting here in absolute frustration. May I complain to you? Thank you.

    1) Got a letter from Brian Henry dated Sept. 11th, saying he hoped I enjoyed the new *Verse*. Which means *Verse* was mailed out sometime before he wrote, and it still hasn't arrived here. I suppose you've gotten your copy by now? Brian explained he only took one of the pieces sent because of the review of my book and mention of me by Simic in his article. But would like to see more work for his next issue.

    2) Got a warm letter from the editor at W. W. Norton, dated August 22, assuming that my copy of the anthology *Micro Fiction* with the permission fee had already been received here. Her letter was sent via Wesleyan, as was the other stuff that never got here. And why Wesleyan and not my home address?

    3) I should have received Miroslav Holub's new *Selected* from Oberlin College by now, as was promised. NOTHING.

    Now let's turn to your problems. First of all, we never write the full "Captain," it's always "The Capt."[1] Also, there are no Grand Masters of the prose poem. There's no way to judge that kind of thing. All the knights at that round table should be considered peers. It may just be that quantity is more important than quality. If this is the case, I've certainly earned the title of His Highness, Little Mr. Prose Poem. I just tacked on His Highness.

    Notice the anthology mentioned above, *Micro Fiction;* there is also Flash Fiction, Instant Fiction, et al. It goes on and on. Each of these anthologies, mostly small, are afraid of the term, prose poem. So what? After a long and tedious meditation, I think "prose poem" is the best way to say it. But as you say, parables, fables, vignettes ... are all part of the mix. There's always a tendency to put poetry on a higher pedestal than fiction. This is probably because traditionally we

---

1. That was Russell's nickname for Robert Bly.

associate poetry with verse, and fiction with prose. And of course the language of verse is more refined than the language of prose. But verse itself does not a poem make. Nor does prose alone a fiction make. In creative writing, poetry and fiction are the two ways of expression. I insist, the shorter a work the more it must depend on poetry thinking. The longer a work the more it must depend on fiction. An epic poem, though in verse, becomes fiction. So let's forget all the la-de-da notions we have of poetry.

Two more near misses ...[2] As I've said before, I don't think it's the form so much as what the prose poem permits the writer to do. The prose poem allows the full play of the imagination where anything is possible, including all kind of dark things, as well as the silly and the whimsical. The "successful" prose poem has the power of a dream, and doesn't give a darn about literary conventions. It creates itself in the moment of its writing. Genre boundary, as you put it, ceases to exist. It is the shape of thought, the way we think, more than what we think. We are in love with our brains because they are in some ways smarter than we are.

You ask for a message from me to your class. Tell them to behave themselves. That's always the best message to young people. But of course they won't. This is why the spanking was invented.

Your most humble servant,

Russell

---

[2]. I was beginning to send out the final version of *Pretty Happy!*

Peter Johnson

November 13, 1996

Dear Peter,

The problem is that language is already an abstraction that tries to represent what we take to be reality. To further abstract it in some *ism* or theory is self-defeating. Imagination is the liberating force. The so-called Language poets remind me of a painter who, instead of painting, spends his time smelling his brushes and easel, thinking that a new age has opened. Any way of writing that needs that much theory about itself (do the so-called Language poets do anything else?) is up the wrong tree, or down the wrong hole.

I try to write beyond the abstraction of language, to find something physical. And you might as well know, Breton turns me off with his manifestos. Writing is personal pleasure, and I'll write anyway I damn well please.

A poem is a mental project and requires one's best mental abilities. We work best when our intellects and imaginations are in harmony at the time of the writing. But I like to go real fast before I ruin what I'm writing by thinking about it. This is not automatic writing. It's a looking for the shape of thought more than the particulars of the little narrative. But why do you have to be a surrealist? Breton didn't invent your imagination. Heck, I consider what I do a homemade art; something made out of all kinds of stuff found around the house. When I entered the "literary" scene I felt very unsure. Everybody seemed steeped in theory, as if they had good reasons to be doing what they were doing. Now we see the so-called Language poets in a kind of cartoon replay of the same scene. You use the example of the bully at the playground. It seems it's not enough to write one's own work, but one must try to tamper and control the work of others. Read Ron (Language poet) Silliman's "The New Sentence." He doesn't scare me.

Charlie Simic sent me his new book *Walking the Black Cat*. It's very Simic, and very good. Gee whiz, Stuart Friebert just published a book, and now Simic, and you'll be publishing one, and here I sit loaded with work.

The Capt. is always the speaker in his poems. I ain't, so I'm allowed to be funny. Humor gives the prose poem dimension. Incidentally, when you get to the Edson section of your course, don't forget why spankings were invented. I think my work is best considered by students who've been properly spanked. Don't forget, I've done a bit of teaching; holding each of my students suspect and spanking-worthy. Particularly the graduate students. I both spanked and handed out MFAs.

I remain your most humble servant,

Russell

Peter Johnson

March 30, 1997

Dear Peter,

You are definitely a surrealist. Of the poets I am aware of, no one is writing like you in these poems; the endless bubbling invention.[1] The nearest poet I can think of is Jim Tate. I wonder what the Capt. would make of them? It's a far cry from anything he could think to write. Or, for that matter, that I could think to write. You have so many startling inventions, almost every sentence. Reading through the poems I would think, why doesn't he develop this one, it would be enough for me to make a whole piece. But then the next sentence is another startling invention; and on it goes. Each invention almost asking to be a poem in itself. And yet, there is a unity in the poems. Not just by theme, or city titles, but the thinking. Something I would like for my work. My books are not really books, but unattached pieces placed together. Every time I write it's as if I have to learn how to write all over again. I'm not talking style. I'm talking disconnection.

Michel's[2] tome promises to be the bible of the American prose poem. I'm looking forward to his book.

The PP (I hope you don't mind my calling the genre PP) is identified as avant-garde, and at the same time it looks easy. "Anything goes," as it were. And anything does go as long as the writer makes it into something. I see your point, we're all little prose poets together. I've never thought of myself as part of a group. When I started publishing I was amazed that anybody saw anything in the pieces. Self-doubt is a wasteful thing.

In my last letter I mentioned that someone of supposed influence had taken an interest in my lack of a publisher. I'm waiting to hear back. I don't want to mess you up at White Pine Press. Some editors resent a writer trying to pack the press with friends. But thanks anyway for the offer. Now I sit here regretting the ms. I sent wasn't

---

1. Prose poems I was writing for *Love Poems for the Millennium*.
2. Michel's Delville's *The American Prose Poem: Poetic Form and the Boundaries of Genre*.

titled *Under Great Light Flooded Clouds,* or, *The Art of the Fugue,* or, *The Secret Graveyeard,* instead of *The Haunted House*. And why didn't I try to arrange the ms. better than the way it came off the disks? I probably don't want to publish. That's the secret I 've been keeping from myself. Self-doubt is a wasteful thing.

You say the new *Journal* is nearly complete. You've been busy. And thanks again for the web business,[3] which will also give the address of the publisher. Oberlin has done no advertising, except in your journal, which they got free. Still, Stuart tells me *TT* is selling well. The prose poem is in.

I don't know if this will reach you before your trip.[4] But if it does, my advice is to let the Capt. have his way with you vis-à-vis the bear-hugging business. There's not much you can do about it, anyway. But no kissing! If we don't have occasion to write before you leave, have a good trip. And remember, you're now Big Mr. Prose Poem. If anybody deserves the title, it's you. One time I think Benedikt wanted the title, but he was either too large, or too small for the station.

Best wishes,

Russell

---

3. Refers to a selection of his work I edited for Mike Neff at *Web del Sol*.
4. Refers to a panel on the prose poem at the 1997 AWP in Washington, DC.

Peter Johnson

April 13, 1997

Dear Peter,

I see you started to write Stamford on your envelope. Please be careful, this is a tricky business.[1]

Sounds like Washington went well. You got your hug, but no kisses, which is proper on a first date. Also got a chance to observe a nasal blockade. Got a three-hour interview with the Capt. Heard my name invoked about 50 times, which must've been boring.

You say the session was well attended. I guess the Capt. helped, but there is also the genre. Interesting too that the Capt. wanted to be part of it, that he's that serious about the genre.

As to your love poems,[2] I'm not sure they would work well as a full-length book. At some point, where, I don't know, the poems might start to blunt each other with their sparks. 24, as you suggest, would make a handsome chapbook. I would suggest you just keep writing the love poems until you feel you've run out creative steam. As I've said before the act of writing is probably everything.

I wouldn't have had the courage to ask the Capt. about his famous tin ear.[3] Speaking of tin, I've been told the Capt. usually wears earmuffs to hide the tin. This tin business has been around for a time, and I find it odd that he should be singled out. Isn't a good much of American poetry tin-earred and tin-brained? I hope you didn't bring up his nasal blockade as part of the interview. Or have I got it wrong, and you meant naval blockade?

Many thanks for your good words for that library display. Mark Twain was, and remains, quite right. My strategy is to stand before a mirror and laugh until I fall.

---

1. Russell had just moved to a new home.
2. Refers to poems that eventually were published in a chapbook by Quale Press, called *Love Poems for the Millennium.* This chapbook ended up as the opening sequence for my *Miracles & Mortifications.*
3. In an interview with Robert Bly I mentioned that some critics have suggested he has a "tin ear."

Having a hard job of settling in here. It feels like a motel that you stay in for a night, knowing that you'll be away the next day for home. I'll look at www.cais.net/aesir/fiction in September. My thanks.

Best regards,

Russell

Peter Johnson

June 16, 1997

Dear Peter,

I'm still here. That's about all I can say.

Not sure you should tell people that you write poetry. Lots of people think of poetry as a sissy sport. Trying to explain what prose poems are is even worse. It comes off as the lazy man's sissy do-nothing. It's best to act as normal as possible. It helps if you think of yourself as a secret agent.

People go to readings because they want to. And a poetry audience is a particularly kind audience. I'm horribly shy, but when one has a script, and one has some faith in the work, it works. Sometimes it can even be exhilarating. Reading funny stuff is a help. When you ask yourself why they bothered to show up, as you say in your letter, just think that they probably had nothing better to do with their evening. Then there are the book signings and the receptions after the readings where people tell you how much they adore you. You'll feel you're not worth all the fuss, but it'll almost feel good. You say of all this that you owe it to your publisher. But you also owe it to yourself. You'll have fun. In our profession it's either drought or flood.

Come to think of it, it's sometimes a good strategy to limp as you approach the reading stand. This focuses the sympathy of the audience. And from then on you can do no wrong. But if this seems too awkward, a speech defect works, too. A lisp, or the inability to pronounce R's. Probably the simplest sympathy getter is to put a cushion inside the back of one's jacket and appear as the humpback of some cathedral. These are tricks of the trade. You'll probably be inventing some of your own as you go along. But as I say, a poetry audience is usually with the reader. The best lighting arrangement is where the light strikes just you, and the audience is hidden from you in the dark. They can see you, but you can't see them. Then it's easy to pretend they're not there. Actually, I've found the bigger the audience the better, it's more impersonal. Small audiences are too intimate, and afraid to laugh at what is so obviously funny. Audiences, unless they know your work, are prepared to sit grim-faced through the reading. Poetry is very serious stuff.

So you have two books coming in September. I imagine the fiction book is more or less *straight* writing. Straight in the sense that it's not prose poems. I should know something about my fate by mid-July. It doesn't look good. Too many unimaginative editors loose in the world.

I don't know why I thought the Bly interview was scheduled for next year. Looking forward, as I always do, to the new issue of the *Journal*.

The word tedious is the clue. When you stop having fun with the love poems you'll know. But from where you are now it's hard to know how far they'll extend. It could well turn out to be a full book. Don't limit yourself, just write. The web thing for this September is fine. After all, it is a gift.

On to the future!

Russell

Peter Johnson

June 30, 1997

Dear Peter,

Thank you for your trouble. Your intro. and selections are fine. Perhaps the web will sell a few *TT*s.

I noticed that in one of the titles you chose, "An Historical Breakfast," the article *A* is used instead of the article *An*. I'm big on articles, my favorite words of our language. Unfortunately there are only three that I know of. Still searching.

I guessed right about your having two ways of writing. I think you mentioned having some background in journalism. I think it's good to have two distinct ways of writing. They define each other. No matter what I write, be it a play or an essay, or even a prose poem, they all seem to be made of the same silly stuff.

True, if you read some poems of attending poets at your readings they'll be flattered beyond critical judgment. Poetry is a social club. But you also have to have a strategy for the rest of the audience. Many times just giving a good reading without any gimmicks will win the day. Of course it doesn't hurt to have a few sympathy-getting backups like a limp or the slight hint of a lisp. Even a few properly timed belches, indicating digestive problems, can bring an audience to a crescendo of approval. You're looking to a busy schedule, teaching and doing the readings. But I rather guess you have the energy having been an athlete in your youth.

Right now my book ms. is in Oberlin. I should know something by mid-July. Problem is that while I have Stuart Friebert's vote, it doesn't count for much because he's retiring. The other four votes are doubtful. Particularly David Young who I think has a more traditional view of the universe than I. He chairs the English Dept.

You say that I'm one of the few people everyone likes to read, even some of the LANGUAGE poets, and that you find it hard to believe I have trouble publishing. It's the lack of courage to send things cold. Anyway, Stuart invited me to send what I sent. Perhaps they'll do it. Perhaps not. I get fan letters all the time asking where they can find my books. Secondhand bookstores. The only thing in print is *TT*.

So you've decided not to have one literary thought during the month of August. Sometimes one gets back to writing after a period of abstinence full of curious things that need to be written. And when August ends it'll be September and you'll have two books coming out. Not bad.

Don't know why, but thought the Bly interview would be running in the coming Vol. It sounds interesting. I'd like to know more about his tin ear. In my kind of writing the ear for common language is all you need. It's an ear made of lead. Just thought, could a "webmaster" also be called a "spider"? And, come to think of it, a spider be called a webmaster?

Glad to hear from you,

Krazy Man

Peter Johnson

July 18, 1997

Dear Peter,

"An Hysterical Lunch" is just right. Many thanks.

Love Poems for the Millennium is a solid work. The inventions work because the language is bold and confident. I know you do a good deal of rewriting, but the poems come off as if you had just thought of them. Perhaps the first poem might be called "Providence." After all it is your home and it fits in with the naming of actual places in the collection. Doing an end poem with the same title as the opening poem is an interesting idea. You start from the beginning, visiting all the places given, returning to where you began. It's a nice way to end the imaginary journey. Think on it, as well as extending the collection. As is, it's solid. You shouldn't have too hard a job placing it. I only wish my work had as much unity.

Small presses have no rule against publishing the same guy again. People worth publishing are not that common. You say you'll need at least 4–5 years to write your next full book. By then anything can happen. White Pine is not the only small press. There's even Oberlin College Press. I've been publishing in *Field* on and off for years. Some years back they asked to see work. The title poem of *TT* was rejected. When it appeared in another magazine, Stuart wrote saying how much he liked it, having forgotten that it had been sent to Oberlin.

Thank you for sending the Bly interview. The questions are good. And the whole presentation will find an interested audience. In fact a plum for the *Journal.* I don't agree with most of his conclusions, or the ways he comes to them. His generalities with all the names and traditions he pulls out of his hat are fun. But it all seems so arbitrary. That business you quote, albeit the "tin ear," that the most important male figures of 20th-century American poetry will be Pound and Bly, is another thing that makes the interview fun to read. But I don't believe the theories behind his poems. I don't believe that writing should have to surround itself with reasons and purposes and all the shoptalk that goes with it. What can be done and expressed in ordinary life shouldn't need to find itself on the poet's page.

For me the way to the imagination begins in utter foolishness. Of course this takes disciplining. The developing of a patience that permits one to sit for periods of time before a keyboard thinking of nothing but foolishness. This isn't easy. Some would call this idleness. And so I, sitting as stated, until I feel entirely emptied of the ability to think, wait for the imagination to open. And if one is lucky, out comes material that amuses its author without social or didactic value. What do you think? Is this too dilettante?

So, with the two books in the offing, and the love poems, which I'm sure someone will grab, you're doing pretty good. I'm still waiting to hear from Oberlin. The longer the wait the more doubtful it seems.

I can't talk into a tape recorder, and that's what people really want, something spontaneous. Not written responses. Many thanks for the enclosures.[1]

Best to you,

Russell

---

1. I had asked to meet up and interview him, but he didn't want to be taped. Eventually I put together questions and answered them with excerpts from his letters, and then we went back and forth adding and subtracting.

Peter Johnson

July 29, 1997

Dear Peter,

Well, my manuscript was returned. If I did something with it, mainly some editing, they would like to see it again. I don't think so.

Meanwhile, I understand from Stuart the press is not faring that well. They're cutting back to just 500 paper and 100 cloth copies. A lot of literary magazines do better than that.

Bly makes me think of a little kid in the candy shop of ideas. His sweet tooth is essentially a romantic one. He sometimes seems unable to distance himself from the idea of an audience. This gives his muse a headache and needing an aspirin. Yet, over the years, he's written many fine poems.

It has been said of Pound-cake that he wrote little that is memorable; the triumph of method over product; not to mention personality, which is a big feature in the mix. With all the bullshit, where are the unique works of art? I think the Cake and his disciples have had a very deadening effect on American poetry. They've been more for how to write poetry than actually writing it. I wonder if other countries get as bogged down in theory as we do?

My prose poem says the hell with theory. But that's a theory too. I suppose one should just close his eyes and write. Another theory. This is why I think it's best to empty one's head, theory or no. I like to imagine my head is a tank of water, something like a fish tank with hair growing on it, which I release down my spinal column into my legs and out of my toes. Then the head is empty and dark. No function at all. Now one is ready.

We might do something by mail vis-à-vis an interview. It won't be as fresh and vulnerable as a tape recorded one. But …

The new *Journal* just arrived! And there's the White Pine announcement of your *Pretty Happy!* with David Ignatow's blurb. He's a good man with a fine body of work. By rough look this might be your best issue; the quality of the work, the fine section of reviews. Still reading. My thanks.

I know how scary proofing can be. One knows the work so well that one might over-read a typo without noticing it. But it's a kick having the galleys in your hands. It means someone is serious about publishing your book. One or two typos might even make a book more authentic. Still, it hurts to have one. More later.

Best,

Russell

Peter Johnson

August 29, 1997

Dear Peter,

Have been thinking about your mail problem. The only answer I can think of is for you to move with no forwarding address, which includes getting a teaching position at another school. Or getting a secretary with a good eye for identifying important mail. Obviously your situation is impossible. And when your book comes out it could even get worse.

The interview idea in correspondence sounds possible. Let's see what happens. Also your idea of having prose poets speak to one of their poems (Commentaries) is a very good idea, it would add to the prose poem's aesthetic base. The only problem with this is, will you be able to hold out for six or seven years more? I think you can, and for many years more. The *Journal* is just too big to walk away from. And a future issue of the Commentaries collected together would make a wonderful issue. Perhaps even a book.[1]

Thought it would be best to publish again with the publisher who did my selected. A sense of continuity, as it were. But at this point in a "career" lacking any continuity, why even think of continuity? Besides, they don't want me.

I wonder if you ever heard back from *Field* about the work you sent. Now that Stuart has retired (last June) I feel rather distant from OC.[2] Yes, they did my selected, and as I shelve the magazines, most of which I haven't looked at for years, I'm surprised to see how many times I published in *Field* over the years. More times than I had remembered.

White Pine Press…? I wonder if they ask a reading fee?

You're going to be asked to write essays because people think you're at the center of what's happening with the prose poem. You've

---

1. 20 years later, that book was eventually published: *A Cast-Iron Aeroplane That Can Actually Fly: Commentaries from 80 Contemporary American Poets on Their Prose Poetry* (MadHat Press, 2019).
2. Oberlin College.

brought all of these miseries on yourself with your *Journal*. Poets are expected to be essayists. I don't know how this got started. I'm not very good at it, but have done a few. One must, or people will think you're just a talented dummy.

Speaking of opinion, all the work in the current *Journal* is mostly high quality. But I was quite taken by Sternberg's "Knit-Wit or the Thread of the Story." For me it is the ideal way to write. The piece is direct and simple and completely self-contained. I reviewed two books of Shapiro's translations of French fables some time ago. He's very good and lively, but he sometimes seems to invent more than an author meant. The title of Sternberg's piece seems like the translator's invention. Its flip tone doesn't feel right to the body of the poem.

By the time you get this you should be home after some marvelous adventure, looking through tons of mail. I'm sorry to be part of the avalanche. Oh, well ...

Best,

Russell

September 9, 1997

Dear Peter,

When we last talked your post-vacation letter had not arrived.

Of the poems you sent to Oberlin, "a few came close." But not close enough. To what?! As I told you, the title piece of my selected was rejected there; published elsewhere, and Stuart happening to see it, wrote me how much he liked it, having forgotten *Field* had rejected it. So I go on showing work only where I'm invited to show work.

Most schools would be proud to have a hot magazine on campus, not to mention a professor who has a book. Obviously what you need is some secretarial service vis-à-vis the mail problem.

Do I understand that you plan to run groups of writers doing commentaries, rather than just one each issue? At any rate, I will prepare something. Would you prefer my using a piece that the *Journal* has carried? Or does that matter?

I'm rethinking my ms. Doing some of the work I planned to do had it been accepted. Pulling pieces, adding pieces; and thinking of using my old ploy of arranging the contents alphabetically. Go from A to Z. Or start at Z and go backward to A. It's all the same. I don't write books, I write pieces that are sometimes collected between covers. Donald Hall once told me that many of my books are really cookbooks. I should have something put together shortly, and will send you a copy. How's this for a title, *Suspension Points*.

As for the correspondence-review thing, why not? We might get something interesting. But please, no questions about my ear, as you know, it's made of gingerbread.

There's no reason why you shouldn't review books in the *Journal*, it's an extension of being an editor. I've done some nutty essays (not very good in the traditional sense), but I don't feel equipped to properly appraise my contemporaries in print. Like anybody else I have opinions, but they are very narrow, and hardly earned.

Anyway, let's go with the commentary thing, which has to be invented, and the interview thing, which has also to be invented.

Everything has to be invented. I've lived on invention. But where is reality? Please forgive this disorganized letter.

Be careful,

Russell

September 27, 1997

Dear Big Mr. Prose Poem,

Sorry for not writing sooner to thank you for *Pretty Happy!* It's a great first book, with a fine send-off by Simic.[1] Of course I know a good many of the poems, but somehow when presented in a physical book, instead of loose, typed sheets, one sees the unity of the writing. And your writing certainly has that. Most good poets have this quality in their books. Though the poems are singular, they reverberate against each other, and form a memorable work.

The photograph of the man in the back of the book is not Peter Johnson, Peter Johnson has a beard. Not only that, but I didn't know you carried a Ph.D. Perhaps you studied with Simic at UNH. Some years back I spent a week there as a visiting something-or-other.

May I assume the website, www.cais.net/aesir/fiction, is the one for me to look for? Is this exactly what to use?

I still intend to send Big Mr. Prose Poem a copy of Little Mr. Prose Poem's ms. He's been sitting here stunned at the possibilities and the lack of them. But I shall be getting on to the commentary thing shortly, which should be a relief. I'd rather be writing something new than looking at stuff already written.

I hope you're happy (at least, pretty happy) with *Pretty Happy!* It's a wonderful first book, and the promise of future books. Your readers will expect it.

And yes, we'll also do that letter interview.

Those three young men on the Plymouth, the two on the left almost look like twins.[2] The one at the left might be you, only he, like the man in the back of your book, doesn't have a beard.

All best,

Little Mr. Prose Poem

---

1. Charles Simic had written an introduction to it.
2. Refers to the cover of *Pretty Happy!*: three eight-year-olds sitting on the hood of an old Plymouth, me being the middle kid.

February 24, 1998

Dear Peter,

Looking at the poems you just sent along, you're right, 30 love poems completes the cycle. You say you're "getting a little sick of Gigi and the narrator." You've put a lot of work into this, all the poems are tersely crafted. No line in any of the poems rests, the invention is endless. And in spite of all the labor involved, the poems all read with a freshness, as if they had just been thought. I don't think more can, or needs be done. It's a unique work as is, except for one more poem to be written. When you finally see it between book covers you won't be disappointed.

I didn't mean to sound like a prima donna vis-à-vis New Rivers Press. If they do some book notices and have some kind of distribution, as you say they do, that's enough to know. I just want a publisher that's somewhat normal. As for funding, you should see the list of financial support in their catalog. With that much tax-free money they could afford to be as daring as they wish. They surely missed a good bet with *Pretty Happy!* Was just looking through it again a few nights ago, and it still holds.

Of course the New Rivers thing is rather moot. As of this writing my ms. has been there 5 weeks. Maybe I should have sent return postage?

Am including 3 pieces for you to consider. They're the best I can do in the love-poem category.

Speaking of which, here's my "lyric essay" title for that *Seneca Review* piece: THE REALITY ARGUMENT: SOME BRIEF NOTES ON HOW THINGS COME TO EXIST, THE QUESTION OF RANDOM SELECTION AND/OR PURPOSEFUL MANUFACTURE, WITH A VIEW TOWARD FINDING A "THEORY OF EVERYTHING."

Good news, "turd" is listed in Webster's. I imagine you were one of those nasty little boys who spent his childhood looking for "dirty" words in every dictionary you met. So spent I my childhood. Where has it gotten us? We're still nasty little boys with whiskers.

You seem to have the future well in hand. I can barely make plans for the past.

Ah, at last a letter from Truesdale.[1] I'm considered there "among the best contemporary American poets." Still, Truesdale wants some outrageous cutting and the addition of other pieces. Some of the cuts make sense, and others don't. "We would all very much like to publish your work." Ah, well ...

Literary taste is so arbitrary. What excites one editor leaves another cold. Still, I'm pleased that I could set your mind at ease vis-à-vis turd. I feel a lot better knowing that turd is an actual word, and not just some vulgar slang. The world feels a little safer, a little more secure with turd on board. We must try to find happiness with little things. Even if one doesn't get a Nobel Prize, one can still have fun writing dirty words.

I wonder what will happen...?

Best,

Russell

---

1. Bill Truesdale, one of the editors at New Rivers Press.

March 7, 1998

Dear Peter,

Your son seems to be aging faster than anyone I know. He was just ten and now, suddenly, he's thirteen. What happened to eleven and twelve?

While the turd piece is not dedicated to you, you are its inspiration. You don't mind my mentioning this in my diary, do you? That's right, I don't keep a diary. So you're safe.

Writing an introduction for three French prose poets is writing an essay.[1] So, whether you like it or not, that makes you an essayist. Your other essay, "I'm Tired," doesn't need anything under the title. The blank page under the title will say it all. That's an essay that will surely be included in many anthologies as a classic of the form.

Your wife is right. The *Journal* is a monster (albeit a well done monster). The more you put into it the more it demands; "a 12-month job," as your wife puts it. And it's too late to invent a 13- or 14-month-year, tradition won't stand for it. A 3-month break couldn't hurt.

I understand you do have a standby publisher for the love poems should the contest thing fail. So in any case the book will see print.

It's encouraging to know that New Rivers is going to do a Jack Anderson prose poem book. You must have a catalog. But I believe New Rivers and I have a lot of road to travel before anything is set, if indeed it ever is. Truesdale has a fairly good eye, to a degree. And some editing suggestions are helpful. We'll see ...

On the "Madam's Heart" problem, my instincts tells me it's right the way I have it. The tense shift of the last paragraph brings it right into the foreground of the present. Even if it is technically wrong, it works. The shifting of tenses is something I've used a number of times.

It's sort of a psychological cubism. But, still, thank you for being the careful editor.

---

1. Refers to an introduction I was writing for *Dreaming the Miracle: Three French Prose Poets: Max Jacob, Jean Follain, and Francis Ponge* (White Pine Press).

John Ashbery invited me to Bard College to read. But looking at the size of the fee and the difficulty of getting there, I don't think so. Ashbery has written prose poems.

Incidentally, I named the thing I sent to New Rivers *The Dear Self.* Too narcissistic? But if one can't be narcissistic about oneself, who can be? It's a dirty job, to be sure, but someone has to do it. Of course this title is subject to change at any moment.

I take it you don't want to rent an apartment at my mother-in-law's place.

Hey, whatever happened to Michel Delville's prose poem book? Was it ever published?

Best,

Russell

March 22, 1998

Dear Peter,

After our telephone conversation, Ashbery wrote a letter of details saying, among other things, what the school could offer and ending with "... I can understand if you found that too little to be bothered with." I don't read for money alone, but the amount does say something. One must live one's own life. No one can do it for us. Everything else was wrong about Bard. A tedious car ride, or a train down to Penn Station, then north along the Hudson River to do a 3:30 afternoon reading to a sparse audience of students. Readings should start at 8:00 in the evening. 3:38 is the cocktail hour. On the other hand I will do a reading for less at the 92nd Street Y with Jim Tate this early winter. First of all, it'll be fun to be with Jim again and, although I've never been to the famous 92nd Street Y, I understand it has a devoted audience. They sent me some literature on its history. They started the readings in 1939, and almost every writer of note has read there.

I think that's a good suggestion, changing the title of the love poems to "Travels with Gigi." I would go with that. The original title seems too abstract and less to the point.

As for an intro, I could try my hand at it. It wouldn't be as gracefully said as Charlie's. I'm not good at straight writing. But, if needed, I could try. I'm always a bit shaky when trying to write something serious.

In the poem "Alaska," why "girl" instead of *gal?* Somehow I want to read, gal. In "New York," near the bottom of the first paragraph you have "the sugared ape." The ape is made of sugar, why not, the sugar ape, it's funnier. The last poem is very good, and fitting. The collection has an enviable unity.

Yes, Patchen tends to be overlooked. It's good that you're including the chapter on him in your next issue. Delville promised me a copy of the finished book. It should be quite interesting. And I'm glad you're giving the book a free ad. Books like that have to be promoted.

He gives the so-called LANGUAGE people a good chapter. Some of them think they're writing the real prose poem. I wonder if they submit work? Ron Silliman really cut me down in an essay ("The New Sentence"). I thought after reading his cruel words that maybe I should switch to verse. But if Bly has a tin ear, mine is couch stuffings.

The back business, I get that every so often. It's painful. We're not made too well in the back. Our fronts are great. But you wanted to walk upright to free your hands for better things than just being feet. We would have been better off had we evolved like insects with six limbs. Or better yet, centaurs with strong horse backs. What fun, galloping over the hills in our iron shoes!

Hope your back is better,

Russell

April 3, 1998

Dear Peter,

I don't know what to expect in NYC, having not be there for years. Your technique of being blindfolded might be the answer. That contest sounds like a big deal. With Gerald Stern being the judge, I guess it is. Jim Tate said he rented a tuxedo for the Pulitzer Prize ceremony. I wonder if you'll have to wear one? Luckily it's something I'll never have to think about.

Another classic essay: "Why I Am a Prose Poet." It's every bit as good as your earlier essay, "I'm Tired." You go right to the heart of things. None of us really knows why we write prose poems. So nothing more needs be said, the blank page under the title says it all. You're breaking new ground.

Maybe Jim will show up for that New York reading, if indeed it happens (it's so far off), wearing a tuxedo. They say once you wear a monkey suit it's very hard not to. Jim sent me his latest book, *Shroud of the Gnome;* not one prose poem.

As for Rosmarie Waldrop, she is poetry. She and Keith are good people. Her interview should be very interesting.[1] I don't place her with those empty theorists like Silliman. Besides, Rosmarie once did a chapbook of mine.

Have retitled my ms. *The Tormented Mirror,* which again is subject to change at any moment. A tormented mirror is the result of subjecting a mirror to extreme narcissism. *The Dear Self* is finally a tormented mirror.

Speaking of narcissism, people publishing their own work, I handset and printed my first pamphlet, which led to my first real book. As you say, it's not unusual for people to publish their own work.

Truesdale in his last letter described Bly as reading his poems "like a rural Lutheran divine." Speaking of Truesdale, I sent him my revised book contents. And that's that. Let's see what he makes of that.

---

1. I had always wanted to interview her but never got around to it.

Peter Johnson

Good luck with the contest. Gerald Stern is a good poet. And I understand a good guy, as well. Win or lose, the book is still a solid work.

Take care,

Russell

May 19, 1998

Dear Peter,

Don't worry, we're all newcomers, and remain so. None of us lives long enough to really understand what we're about. All we can do is to do what we do, hoping it will do.

I've seen good patches of Michelle Delville's book, it'll be fun to see the whole thing with you quoted on the back cover. Back covers are getting to be a habit with you. *The Party Train,* and now this. His book could have historical importance. No joke.

You have no choice but to continue the *Journal.* You couldn't let all that pretty, new stationery go to waste. The time you've given to the *Journal* is not lost. It's all part of being involved in and with the American prose poem. There is such a beast. I know I feel a lot less isolated since the *Journal* began to be published.

Of New Rivers, finally heard from Truesdale. They need more time, as if they haven't had more than enough time. And if I did publish there it would be delay and distraction, distraction and delay. I haven't the patience. I'll let it slide for a while, and then…?

The proofs are okay. There's an extra dot at the end of "Madam's Heart"; not important, and my fault at that.

I want to write something for your intro.[1] Will get on that shortly. So things move along apace.

Best,

Russell

---

1. Russell wrote a preface for *Love Poems for the Millennium.*

June 5, 1998

Dear Peter,

The first line of your May 29 letter saying that you removed the last dot from "Madam's Heart"[1] sounds more like a medical procedure than a typographical correction.

Living intimately with a prosecutor is like living life as a defendant. It should bring a new excitement to the marriage. Congratulations to your wife.

Your first review,[2] and a good one. Bill Stobb says a lot of the right things for your book; a lot of the right things that should be said for the genre itself. It's not enough just to publish. One needs some reviews, some feeling that one's book is out there, and that someone has read it. *NDQ* looks like a quality magazine.

I'm enclosing the introduction for *Love Poems for the Millennium*. I hope you won't feel it's too silly or trivial.

That's interesting that the Capt. read a new prose poem to you over the phone. It can sometimes be little frightening to hear a prose poem coming out of the receiver of one's telephone. As you say, I too "have had nothing but good experiences with him." We've even read together. The poster of that reading hangs in my writing room. Obviously he thinks your opinion is important. Somehow you've intimidated him.

Needless to say, as of this writing, nothing from New Rivers. Maybe I died?

Some important information: Martha of Martha's Vineyard is, or was, Martha Gosnold, and Ann of Ann Arbor is, or was, Ann Allen. Nice stuff to know.

Hope the mini vacation served well.

Best,

Russell

---

1. One of his poems I published.
2. A review of *Pretty Happy!* in the *North Dakota Quarterly*.

June 16, 1998

Dear Peter,

Got your letter. That must mean I'm still alive. Thank you for reminding me. I was making funeral arrangements.

Yes, your version of the intro. is neater.[1] And had I known it would have a title, I would have chosen that one. However, and I hate to say this (too many opinions can unsettle one's nerves), *Love Poems for the Millennium* seems a bit heavy. Of course the word *millennium* is attractive. Well, you're the poet and, by coincidence, the author.

Anyone whose work appears in an anthology, or a work like Delville's, is automatically sent a copy. It's a traditional courtesy and honorarium. But you don't think the Capt. or Simic got theirs either. Surely Gertrude got hers! I am rather curious about the size of my picture on the cover.

I'm trying something I've never tried before. I wrote to a publisher offering my book. As for New Rivers, I'm doing nothing about that, just letting it ride. Figuring if Peter can offer his work without false modesty, why can't I? In this matter you've become my role model. Life is really too short to baby one's neuroses. There's nothing wrong about getting one's show on the road by asking me or Simic to intro. your books; or even the Capt. Although, Simic and the Capt. carry more weight than I do, something is better than nothing.

Speaking of coincidences, if one's water heater is going to die and flood the cellar,[2] it will always wait for its folks to be out of town. We don't have natural gas service here. So we have an amazingly small oil burner which heats the house very well, and is also the water heater. Most of my life I've struggled with rusted-out, gas fueled water heaters. You say the other household fixtures still work. However, it might be a good caution never to leave them again.

---

1. Russell's preface to my *Love Poems for the Millennium*.
2. My wife and I went to Martha's Vineyard, where I broke a tooth and came home to a flooded cellar and a grumpy house painter.

You probably did yourself a service by flossing. That tooth, unbeknownst to you needed servicing quite badly. It's frightening when a piece of one's body breaks off like that. But then you realize it's not a finger or something else, and that you still have 31 teeth left. One has only 10 fingers, and only 1 of something else; I mean if one had 32 fingers, or 32 you-know-whats, it wouldn't matter all that much.

Your house-painting story sounds like a TV sitcom. And all the guy really wanted was a kiss.

Martha-of-the-vineyard and I used to sit around together drinking the fermented blood of her grapes. She told me nothing's real, that we are as ghosts drifting among our possessions. I said, but Martha dear, your vulva is as solid as any Volvo. With that she slapped my face and kicked me off her island. Since then I have been drifting in and out of consciousness.

Would it be fair to say that your wife is a prosecutrix, as in aviatrix?

Actually, you sound spiritually up and rested in spite of the assaults on tooth and home, Martha was good for you. I take it you had the good sense while in her vineyard not to mention her vulva.

Best,

Russell

Truths, Falsehoods, and a Wee Bit of Honesty

June 28, 1998

Dear Peter,

There's no reason why your book shouldn't have more preface pages than poems. With prose poetry anything is possible. You're breaking new ground as you have with your remarkable titles-only essays.

Love Poems for the Millennium will have a publisher dedicated to the prose poem. That'll be a first. I just sent Gian[1] some work for his oddly named magazine. He complained that he had sent the Capt. a couple of letters asking for work with no reply. I guess prose poem writers would rather try your *Journal* first.

A friend of mine, some years back, sent me his book of translations of Breton's *Earthlight,* published by Sun & Moon. In the back of that book is a list of some of their other books, which looked very promising. So I sent a letter, but got no reply. Perhaps they've moved, or they're just not interested. Is that possible? It doesn't matter, the mood has passed.

Sorry that prosecutrix didn't work for you. We may have to go to prosecutress as in actress. After this I've run out of ideas. Still think trix sounds cuter.

I'm a Man[2] just came in the mail …

June 29. Thank you, the stories are sad and funny. I had forgotten how effecting fiction can be, but I'm going to stay with the prose poem. As far as I know, these are very well written. They have a reality that holds the reader. But of course, this is what I have against fiction; becoming imprisoned in a story; something you can't get out of until you know the end. So your tales work, and are better written than many prose poems. Perhaps I'll send you *Gulping's Recital*[3] one day, one of my early stabs at fiction.

---

1. Gian Lombardo, prose poet and editor of Quale Press.
2. A book of short stories I had just published with White Pine Press.
3. One of Russell's novels.

Anyway, you're doing good. Two books published, and one in the oven. Hope I didn't bore you too much with all this crap.

Best,

Russell

August 22, 1998

Dear Peter,

Volume 7, WOW! No wonder you're ready for a nervous breakdown. Coordinating all that material, and writing some of it yourself. The perfectly chosen David Ignatow cover poem; the format cover design coincidentally befitting the occasion. Which must include William Matthews, whose death was *truly,* using the oft used word, untimely. One feels that David lived long enough at least to get most of his work written, assuming that to be the poet's purpose. Perhaps our real purpose is to return to an age "When People Could Fly."[1] Perhaps that's what death is all about?
   ... That's a nice feature on Patchen, the commentaries, the many and full book reviews, and of course the interview with the Capt.; mainly the new prose poems which are the flesh and bone of the issue. You have outdone yourself. I shall be poring over this issue for many a day, and then some. Many thanks.
   Still working on our interview.
   I suddenly notice three books on the prose poem, reviewed by Delville. One begins to feel that the free form is gradually being webbed in by a terminology that neglects the very spirit of the prose poem. I suppose the main purpose of academics is to put everything into academic coffins. I'm getting tired of all these johnny come-latelys messing with my prose poem. It just seems suddenly the prose poem is getting too much attention from people who know nothing about the genre. It's grotesque. The prose poem is becoming a monster.
   Please forgive the above. I still love you.

Russell

Little Mr. Angry Prose Poem

---

1. Refers to a prose poem written by Morton Marcus.

September 3, 1998

Dear Peter,

I wouldn't know where to begin with that AWP assignment, even though I've been thinking about the prose poem so much vis-à-vis our interview that my head is practically a morgue of dead brain cells.

An overview of prose poems is almost impossible. They really have only one thing in common. They're written in prose. From then on anything goes; even Ronald Silliman with his new "prose poem." Just had a funny thought. Maybe when Benedikt reemerges he will have been transformed into a Language poet.

You say you have contradictory thoughts about the prose poem. Maybe you should write your AWP essay in the form of a dialogue with yourself. Use the contradictions as talking points. Remember, as the editor of the hottest prose poem magazine in America, it's assumed that you know everything there is to know about the prose poem. But it's easier than you might think, because no one knows anything about them. The obvious history of the prose poem is very available. But doing something more with it is the difficult part, if indeed that's what's called for. The Capt. shoots from the hip. That's about what I do, having nothing to lose. But you probably don't want to be too reckless. You could well work in your experience editing the *Journal*, which is really cutting edge in the prose poem world. You're right, an empty page with just a title at the top won't work this time. Maybe this essay business will send you running back refreshed to writing prose poems again. You say the chapbook exhausted you, but that's worthy exhaustion.

I've forgotten the date when this draft of the interview should be in Providence. Still working on it, and may be overdoing it. But the "reclusive" Edson has a few things to say.

Good idea, "Best Of" for Volume 10, if you get through Volumes 8 and 9. As you say, life is just one big downhill sled looking for a convenient tree. Best to hold tight and hope for the best.

Wheeee!

Russell

Peter Johnson

October 14, 1999

Dear Peter,

Just a note. I know you're busy. Brooke Horvath's review (*Texas Review*) is excellent.[1] But I don't agree with saying you were a genius "for at least 5 minutes." As the famous saying about celebrity goes, I would give you at least 15 minutes. One of the strengths of your poems, which I think is the key, is your language. The imagination needs a language that at least seems to believe what it carries. I get stuff sent here, and I can tell that most of it is written by people who really write line poems trying to write the poem in prose. I never tried to write verse, and I think you said you come from fiction. Maybe that's the best training. Fiction finding poetry.

Michel sent me his book with a nice letter asking if I'd like to see an essay he wrote. He seems unhappy with the epilogue to his *American Prose Poem,* and this essay might be somewhat of a remedy. Who knows? He also said that the book had won the SAMLA Award. Not knowing what that is, I congratulated him anyway. I didn't mention you had sent a copy of the book, he seemed to go to so much trouble to send it all the way from Belgiun.

I should think the love poems have been proofed by now.

Best,

Russell

---

1. Review of *Pretty Happy!*

November 30, 1999

Dear Peter,

Briefed through the interview and it looks okay. I'll look at it again; spotted a few typos. But the basic interview is done. As you say, we've plenty of time, so I want to give it a more careful look. A brief intro? Perhaps best from your pen since you are host of the interview. Wish we were publishing it next week.
   You don't have to thank me. The interview was fun to do. I should thank you for thinking it worth doing.
   Am finding lately, instead of writing out of "pure" imagination, which is the spirit of the prose poem for me, it's also fun to write to recognizable ideas. My instinct with prose poems has always been to write things that were complete little systems almost totally invented.
   Speaking of which, Gian wrote that when your love poems went to press the figures on the cover were fully clothed. Somehow their clothes didn't make it through the printing.
   Some days back Jim Tate called, and among other things he mentioned that he had written a number of prose poems lately, and that he'd be sending you something.
   You're right about the word honor. Only the king of Sweden is allowed to have that word attached to his august person. Hey, he rules by "divine right!" A wonderful tradition that makes his throne just an inch lower than God's.
   Please don't worry about the interview. It stands.

Most humbly,

Russell

Peter Johnson

April 11, 1999

Dear Peter,

Please forgive my slowness. This'll be the first letter written since falling ill. All kinds of unanswered mail piled up here.

But to attend to business: I signed and had my wife mail the interview proof back to AWP[1] the very day you called. Had meant to call you back, but time just seems to flow whether one is using it or not.

Actually, my brain has not fully returned. Surprisingly it fails like any other organ, being only flesh. You didn't really think it was divine, did you? It's not much different than a kidney or a liver. It lives in a shell made of bone, much like a clam. I long to be writing again!

The 92nd Street Y sent a car for me, otherwise I should have missed reading with Jim Tate. There's no luxury more than being driven about in a chauffeured car.

The new work you sent is very good. You say you'll wait until fall to start hitting some magazines with it. Of course an author always sees his work from the other side of the mirror. From my side, the work reads well enough for print. I see no reason not to be sending it out now. It sometimes helps to see one's work objectified in someone else's print. Magazines are, after all, experimental texts. When it comes time for a book one can always make changes without any loss of grace. Reading through your poems makes me nostalgic for my own writing; the creative itch to make something. As of now I am not able to compose anything, no matter how foolish.

You're doing good,

Russell

---

1. My interview with Russell originally appeared in the *AWP Chronicle*.

February 24, 2001

Peter,

Got your e-mailed *Eduardo* poems, many thanks. Eduardo is a psychological monster of strange desire. I imagine he's the secret you, telling all your secrets disguised as poems. This is one of the best reasons to be a writer; to go naked into the world while wearing everything one knows; like the secret of an onion, which is that there is no onion, only layers and layers into nothingness, just the peeler's tears. And even they evaporate. Nothing keeps, nor perhaps was ever even there.

Eduardo might want more than two more poems to be completed. I would do the two poems and set it aside for other writing, and let a little time pass before looking at it again. You may finally see Eduardo as a book. Forget the word random, it doesn't apply.

So it's definite with the Capt.[1] I guess he's the one drawing all the responses to the conference. Good enough. Meanwhile, I have two Arizona dates back-to-back in April; two weeks of it. Lots of money, and lots of enthusiastic strangers; that's the hard part. One has to be dignified and gracious, quelling the urge to puke and scream, anybody could write my crap.

Got the *Journal*'s death certificate in the mail. Everybody's going to miss it, it gave center and movement to the prose poem. The *Journal* is probably responsible for making the prose poem almost legitimate; something worth doing.

Anyway, I'm sending you my new book.[2] Of course I shall expect a free ad in the *Journal!*

Best,

Russell

---

1. Robert Bly had to agree to do a week-long conference on the prose poem with Russell, me, and Nin Andrews at Great River Arts in Putney Vermont.
2. *The Tormented Mirror* was eventually published by Ed Ochester in the Pitt Poetry Series.

IF CATULLUS WERE A PROSE POET

If Catullus Were a Prose Poet

If Catullus were alive now, he would certainly be writing prose poems. Sure, one can find many prose poems that are deftly written quiet nature studies or deep philosophical musings. But a quick glance at the major figures of prose poetry suggests that the genre has always attracted the bad boys and girls of the poetry world. These are the poets who want to push thematic and linguistics boundaries, the smart-asses and punks who have influenced so many of us. What follows is a prose-poem translation of Catullus's famous Lesbia poem, along with a commentary. When I am old and infirm, I hope to spend my last days translating more of Catullus, revisiting my Latin roots, while, hopefully, laughing my ass off.

Weep, you Loves and Cupids

Catullus (84–54 BC)

Lugete, o Veneres Cupidinesque,
et quantum est hominum venustiorum:
passer Marcusuus est meae puellae,
passer, deliciae meae puellae,
quem plus illa oculis suis amabat.
nam mellitus erat suamque norat
ipsam tam bene quam puella matrem,
nec sese a gremio illius movebat,
sed circumsiliens modo huc modo illuc
ad solam dominam usque pipiabat.
qui nunc it per iter tenebricosum
illuc, unde negant redire quemquam.

>   at vobis male sit, malae tenebrae
>   Orci, quae omnia bella devoratis:
>   tam bellum mihi passerem abstulistis
>   o factum male! o miselle passer!
>   tua nunc opera meae puellae
>   flendo turgiduli rubent ocelli.

Weep, you Loves and Cupids, and all who live for loveliness. My girl's sparrow is dead. My darling girl's sparrow that she loved more than her eyes, for it was honey sweet and knew her better than any girl knew her mother. That bird wouldn't leave her lap, but popping up, here and there, peeped only for its mistress. Now it travels a gloomy journey from where no one returns. But a curse on you, evil shades of Orcus, you who devour all pretty things. You've made off with my pretty sparrow. Oh, evil deed! Oh, wretched sparrow! Because of you my girl's eyes are reddened and heavy with tears.

COMMENTARY

It's surprising so much has been written on Catullus considering how little we know about his life. He is attractive to the classicist interested in how he imitates and subverts Greek models, yet also cherished by the lovelorn and alienated who, sometimes mistakenly, look to the Lesbia poems and invectives during anxious and angry moments. But primarily Catullus is a comic poet and one very well suited to our postmodernist times, especially in his merging of high and low subjects and discourses. In the above poem, commentators have pointed out how the elevated language of the opening is followed by a slang expression, and how diminutives toward the end simulate an odd kind of baby talk. There is also a somber reference to Orcus (Death), yet it is surrounded by playful language, the line "*sed circumsiliens modo huc modo illuc*" imitating the bird's movements.

    This kind of mischievous juxtaposition and word play drives the poem, making it impossible to see it, as some do, as a lamentation on all-consuming Death, just as it is difficult to believe Catullus was unaware of the sexual connotations of Lesbia's sparrow. He is using an ancient form, the threnody or funeral dirge, and undercutting it by substituting a sparrow for a hero or nobleman, then further undercutting it through exaggeration in order to simultaneously sympathize with and tease Lesbia. What makes Catullus very much our contemporary is how his "I" becomes ironic through exaggeration, whether he is comparing the number of his kisses to the sands in the Libyan desert (VII) or asking Ipsithilla to prepare for nine consecutive copulations (XXXII). This kind of conceit, a staple of all great love poetry, renders the speaker attractive and suspect at the same time. On one hand, the hyperbole idealizes the lover and beloved; on the other hand, the inflated posturing suggests an overblown sense of self-importance, which, I'm sure, Catullus's inner circle of readers appreciated.

Admittedly, the speaker of the Lesbia poems often seems genuinely tortured and jealous; likewise in the invectives, he appears to be honestly infuriated, as when he threatens to sodomize Aurelius or Furius for criticizing his erotic verse (XVI). But, still, in most of Catullus's love poems and invectives there is often a hint of self-mockery, as if any event in Catullus's life exists mostly so he can verbally perform for his beloved, his friends, and himself. Consequently, if we refuse to look at Catullus's "I" ironically, all we are left with are the romantic overstatements and rants of a petulant schoolboy, and we ignore the complexities of his wit and style—the very reasons we still read him today.

Acknowledgements

"Truths, Falsehoods, and a Wee Bit of Honesty," from *Crossroads: Journal of the Poetry Society of America.*

"The Prose Poem and the Problem of Genre," from *Plume.*

"The Prose Poem and the Comic: On Russell Edson's 'The Manual of Sleep,'" from *Green Mountains Review.*

"Parable vs. Prose Poem: Lawrence Fixel's 'Flight Patterns,'" from the *Collected Poetry and Prose of Lawrence Fixel,* edited by Gerald Fleming.

"Introduction to *Sentence: A Journal of Prose Poetics,* Volume 4."

"My Ten Favorite Books, At Least for This Week," from *The Poet's Bookshelf: Contemporary Poets on Books That Shaped Their Art,* edited by Peter Davis and Tom Koontz.

"Art of the Prose Poem: Interview with Russell Edson," originally published in the *AWP Chronicle.* Later republished in *The Prose Poem: An International Journal,* Volume 8.

"Art of the Prose Poem: Interview with Robert Bly," from *The Prose Poem: An International Journal,* Volume 7.

"Interview with Peter Johnson by Steve Frech," from *Another Chicago Magazine.*

"Interview with Peter Johnson by David Cass," from *Web del Sol.*

"Interview with Peter Johnson by Jamey Dunham," from *Sentence: A Journal of Prose Poetics.*

"If Catullus Were a Prose Poet," published under a different title in *Poetry Daily.*

Special thanks, as always, to Marc Vincenz, excellent poet, editor, and, most important, friend of the prose poem.

About the Author

PETER JOHNSON's prose poetry has been awarded an NEA and two Rhode Island Council on the Arts fellowships. His second book received the James Laughlin Award from The Academy of American Poets. New books are: *Old Man Howling at the Moon* (MadHat Press, 2018), *A Cast-iron Aeroplane That Can Actually Fly: Commentaries from 80 Contemporary American Poets on Their Prose Poetry,* editor (MadHat Press, 2019), and *Truths, Falsehoods, and a Wee Bit of Honesty: A Short Primer on the Prose Poem, with Selected Letters from Russell Edson* (MadHat Press, 2020). A book of short stories, *Shot,* will be published in January of 2021 (MadHat Press). He is a Professor Emeritus at Providence College. More about Peter and his work can be found at peterjohnsonauthor.com

Made in United States
North Haven, CT
06 November 2022